# Feng Shui

## The Key Concepts

## ACKNOWLEDGMENT

Many people have helped in the production of this book. However I would like to make special mention of the advice and editing skills of Shelley Neller with the original manuscript and the final checking by Geoff Piper in the frantic days before going to the printer.

# Feng Shui

THE KEY CONCEPTS

*George Birdsall*

*Published by*
*Waterwood Management Proprietary Limited*
*(A.C.N. 003 529 057)*
*P.O. Box 278 Spit Junction, N.S.W.*
*Australia, 2088.*

*First Published 1995*
*Reprinted 1995, 1996*

*A Catalogue Record of this book is available from the National Library of Australia*

*ISBN 0 646 23358 0*

*Edited by Shelley Neller*
*Cover Design by Ingrid Urh, Reno Design Group*
*Illustrations by Wayne Boyd, Reno Design Group*
*Printed by Australian Print Group*
*Wholesale Book Distribution Enquiries 0412-170 687*
*Feng Shui Enquiries 02 - 9751 1016*

# DEDICATION

*This book is dedicated to all the people who have inspired this book's production.*

# CONTENTS

# Preface

I first became aware of feng shui about 10 years ago when a $20 million project I was building in Sydney's Chinatown district was assessed by a Chinese geomancer and feng shui practitioner. His major recommendations included the realignment of the escalators so that the "wealth did not flow out" and a delay of one week before we could start demolition and construction. We were allowed to start on a particular day, at a particular time and to demolish only three bricks before going off to have a celebratory lunch with Chinese dignitaries. We started proper demolition the next day.

Like most Westerners this seemed strange to me at the time as my focus was on more practical concerns, but we went along with it as we were advised that the Chinese community would not lease a building with bad feng shui.

My subsequent experiences have demonstrated that feng shui can have a clear and definable use in business development, commercial building, home and interior design in modern western culture. It can be applied in both new and existing buildings, often without significant cost. In buildings where the principles have been applied people have reported "coincidental" changes to various aspects of their fortune and health.

The aim of this book is to provide a starting point for anyone with an interest in feng shui or Chinese geomancy. It has been written to give the layman an understanding of feng shui and bridge the gap to the more advanced books written by various authors. It has come about because I have been constantly asked during my feng shui seminars and consultations to recommend a book on feng shui, which could clearly explain the key concepts to anyone with a interest in the subject.

I hope this book will inspire you to apply the key concepts of feng shui in ways that may allow your life to flow more easily. What feng shui and geomancy provide is one method for enhancing your life. Do not expect feng shui to give you all the answers to your problems. If you apply it wisely, with some humour and discernment, you can achieve better results than if you are too serious or greedy about the application. I would also add that even greater benefits often appear to flow for people who are simultaneously developing the physical, mental and spiritual aspects of their lives.

The bottom line is to trust your intuition, enjoy applying feng shui and geomancy and use this ancient knowledge prudently in your modern situation. Remember: "Put a little feng shui and geomancy into your life, not your life into feng shui and geomancy".

*George Birdsall*

# Introduction

Feng shui is an ancient Chinese system of rules, concepts and principles that endeavours to explain the impact on people's lives, of the layout and design of their homes and businesses, and the environment around them. It is about creating a living and working environment that is balanced and harmonious. In Chinese language feng shui literally means "wind" and "water". The "wind" provides the movement or flow of universal energy or chi which affects everything. The "water" provides the container or receiver of chi. Feng shui principles are designed to harmonise the wind and water influences.

Feng shui is also known as Chinese geomancy. It encompasses what Eastern philosophy refers to as the "chi" flow or energy flow within a building. This concept is not dissimilar to the chi flow within the human body upon which acupuncture is based. According to this philosophy if chi flows evenly through your body, you are generally healthy. Therefore if chi gently flows through your home or business, then your life appears to flow more easily and "luck, fortune or good coincidences" come your way.

One purpose of applying feng shui concepts is to create a place where you want to spend time, rather than a one from which you are constantly trying to escape because something doesn't feel right. If the places where you spend a lot of time feel pleasant, this will have an affect on your general attitude to life, and on everyone who comes to your home or business.

You may intuitively know something feels wrong about a place, but are at a loss to explain those feelings. You may also have observed situations in which peoples' luck or health altered following a change of home or business premises. Feng shui proposes some answers to why these situations occur. It also provides some simple solutions to improve the flow, balance, harmony, wealth, health, fame, relationships, career and creative aspects of people's lives. Seemingly inconsequential feng shui adjustments can sometimes radically affect how you feel about your surroundings.

Exactly why feng shui works, continues to be a mystery to our twentieth century minds and anyone approaching the use of this knowledge from a logical or "left brain" approach is bound to be disappointed. Feng shui involves a more "right brain" approach, using intuition and feelings. Remember that the application of feng shui principles are based mostly on observation, reflection and common sense. Feng shui offers us techniques to express what we are feeling intuitively about a place. So when you walk into a place which doesn't "feel" right, instead of dismissing that intuitive feeling, you should be able to look around and assess what might be contributing to your feelings of unease. If it is a place that you can change, then make the appropriate feng shui alterations, and then observe over time the impact of these changes, whether profound or subtle. Also note how your friends or customers react. Many people report that after making feng shui changes, friends or clients have walked into their homes or business and insisted that the place has been renovated, painted or had some other major physical change. The visitors can feel the change, but because of their conditioning, they are looking for physical signs of the change, rather than understanding that subtle inexpensive changes can also have an impact. This idea of the impact of the visible as well as the invisible environment on our lives will be discussed in chapter three.

The following chapters contain stories about the significant changes experienced by various clients after a feng shui consultation. However, not everyone has had large changes occur, and some of the changes are so subtle, that without someone else independently commenting about the changes, you may not even notice them. Sometimes the application of feng shui has done no more than make the persons house feel like a home or allow them to get a good night's sleep.

This book does not delve into great depth about every situation that could possibly arise, as it would be impossible to do that; rather it is intended as an introduction to the key concepts so that you can begin to apply them to your place in an intuitively personal way. Rather than asking you to adhere to the rule book for specific solutions to every feng shui problem you encounter, this book should be seen as a basis and guideline for the application of this knowledge.

The book begins by reviewing the history of feng shui and geomancy and the philosophical approach on which it is based. The key concepts of feng shui are outlined in the remainder of the book. Appendices B and C summarise information on how Electromagnetic Fields and Natural Earth Energies may also be affecting the "feel" of your home or business and the health of its occupants. Appendix D includes information on dowsing techniques that allow the energy or chi in your place to be found and adjusted more easily.

# 1

# *History of Feng Shui and Geomancy*

The study of feng shui attempts to explain how any place, but in particular your home or business, can have an impact on your life. People often comment that "ever since we moved into a new home, everything has improved in our lives", or that "everything has gone wrong." It is, as if the choice of a home has had a dramatic influence on their fortunes.

Our homes, and the land on which they are situated, can sometimes be the source of unapparent stresses, and these can have a dramatic impact on our lives. Over time, these stresses may cause health, wealth, relationship and creative problems for the people who live or spend time in this place.

Following a recent public introductory talk on feng shui

and geomancy, a gentleman commented that "it now makes sense why I've lost everything since I moved into my latest home four years ago." He had always had plenty of money, but during the years in that home, everything had gone wrong and he was nearly bankrupt! What was so "wrong" with the home? In terms of feng shui, he had a toilet in the "wealth" corner of his home! (This concept and the solutions will be explained later in the book). Six months later, after making the suggested feng shui corrections to balance the energy in his home, his finances had stabilised and begun to improve. Intuitively he knew something was wrong, but until he heard about feng shui, he didn't know what he could do.

This man's story typifies the kinds of stories people from all walks of life have expressed during consultations and seminars over the past few years. It is as if our intuition is telling us that something doesn't feel right, but our rational, logical education has trained us to ignore those intuitive feelings.

## INTUITION AND OUR ANCESTORS

One way of explaining intuitive feelings about a place is to consider the way we live today, compared with our ancestors, and then to expand this understanding of the energies of a place in terms of feng shui.

In Westernised Industrialised societies, it has become gradually easier to pass on responsibility for many aspects of our lives to others. We go to the supermarket for food or to the doctor for medical advice. Our lives are generally comfortable, we live in a world full of gadgets, appliances, electricity and telecommunications. The emphasis on survival that occupied our ancestors lives has been superseded by a technologically sophisticated existence. However, it is becoming apparent in a number of ways that progress has its price.

We appear to have lost touch with many skills that our ancestors used for their day to day survival. In particular, the ability to trust and use our intuition or gut feelings, has faded for many people in our modern world. Often we experience these intuitive feelings in our homes, offices or shops, but if we get a slightly uneasy feeling about that place, we dismiss it as irrelevant because we cannot see any visible evidence to justify that feeling.

It is only when we go into a place and feel physically ill or frightened that we will take action. So we haven't lost our intuition completely, but often our ability to trust and interpret these more subtle feelings is clouded by our dependency on the modern, physical and material world.

Sometimes the most subtle feeling of unease can be a sign that a place is out of balance energetically, and if we spend a lot of time in this place, it may have an impact on our lives.

Our ancestors explained these intuitive feelings about a place in terms of what we can refer to as geomancy. Geomancy has been used in many cultures under various names. The Hawaiian Kahunas, American Indians and Australian Aborigines have all used an understanding of geomancy to facilitate their survival.

"Geo" means earth and "mancy" means the divination or messages from the earth. Divination of the earth originally derived from the concept that future decisions about peoples existence could be interpreted from the pattern created when a handful of soil was cast on the earth.

For the earliest nomadic people, the ability to read the messages from the earth was important as they had to look for signs of weather conditions, movement of animals and indications of where they could find food and water.

With the development of farming and agriculture these skills were still vital. They had to deduce the best time and place to plant crops, and the safest place to sleep. These decisions blended experience, intuition and an ability to read the land to find the most auspicious place to carry out these tasks.

In the above definition, our modern interpretation of the term "earth" is extended from the original idea of the soil under our feet to mean anything from the built or natural environment which can have an impact on us.

Early geomancy knowledge was part of an oral story-telling tradition that has in many cases been lost due to the effects of modernisation and industrialisation. However one way this ancient feel for the earth can still be divined in our modern world is by rediscovering the concepts of feng shui which were first documented about 2000 years ago.

*Figure 1.1 Ancient Chinese Geomancers*

## FENG SHUI OR CHINESE GEOMANCY HISTORY

Traditional chinese geomancy was taught verbally and passed through the generations in various forms for thousands of years, until feng shui was mentioned in Guo-Pu's book, *Zhang Shu or The Book of Burial* during the Jin Dynasty (276-420 AD.)

The early feng shui concepts developed from the belief that the "afterlife" of the ancestors, played a role in their descendants physical existence on earth. Feng shui principles were applied to the landscape in order to find the most auspicious place to bury one's ancestors. The Chinese believed that if they buried their ancestors in an auspicious place, then they would look after them during their lives, and thus ensure that their lives were also auspicious. They respected the invisible, as well as the physical world. This attitude did not stand independently of other customs of the times, but was integrated into daily life.

Another part of the history of feng shui is explained by legend. Legend tells us that the philosopher Fu Hsi, while meditating on the banks of the Lo River in Northern China, noticed a tortoise emerge from the river with a series of solid and broken lines on its back. He suddenly realised that the entire universe was reflected in the orderly markings, which were arranged in eight combination sets of three lines, some broken (yin) and some solid or unbroken (yang). The markings symbolised heaven and earth, fire and water, mountain and lake, wind and thunder. This pattern is known as the Early Lo Map or Heavenly Sequence.

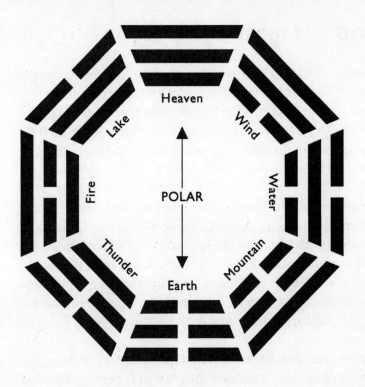

*Figure 1.2   Early Lo Map*

This information formed a philosophical basis for feng shui and other eastern philosophical concepts such as the bagua, I Ching (the book of change), yin/yang concepts Nine Star Ki, Five Element Theory and Taoism among others. The basic concepts of some of these ideas are expressed in Appendix A.

## FENG SHUI TODAY

The combination of the principles of finding an auspicious place to bury your ancestors and later developments of the lo map to form the bagua (which will be explained in chapter five) form the basis for feng shui as it is applied today. In particular it applies to the places where people live and work.

Feng shui is also based on a recognition of the "universal energy" or chi, qi or ki flow within any place and "dragon lines of chi in the landscape". For simplicity we will use the term "chi" or "energy" throughout this book. Again, we cannot see this chi, but by applying the principles of feng shui you can enhance the flow of chi to create a more harmonious place.

Throughout this book, the concept of energy and energy flow will unfold. It may be difficult to accept at first, but as you try some of the corrections and adjustments in your own home or business, you may notice changes in the feel of the place or in some aspect of your life. Our logical brains often dismiss the changes as mere coincidences, but how many "coincidences" does it take to convince us that the invisible world, on which many Eastern philosophies are based, can have just as big an influence on us as the physical world?

It is interesting to note that in Hong Kong the success or failure of businesses is often attributed to a respect for its location relevant to the "dragon lines of chi on the landscape". Buildings like the Hong Kong Regent Hotel have been specifically designed so as not to interrupt the flow of chi on the landscape and have operated successfully since opening. Some unsuccessful buildings have had to be modified at substantial cost to their owners when they have ignored this respect for the natural environment.

## PLACES OF POWER

The Chinese people were not the only culture to recognise the energy in a place and dragon lines of energy in the landscape. Many ancient peoples acknowledged that there were earth energies which could be harnessed in various ways to help give a definition to their lives.

In the British Isles this respect for the energetic power of the earth or land is powerfully evident at places like Stonehenge, Avebury and other sacred sites.

These sites were often linked in various ways to healing, fertility, seasonal festivals and other ceremonies. It was as if they were a focus of the heavenly and earth energies for man, a blending of the so-called universal energy or chi.

This link between man, the earth and the heavens is persuasively evident in the geomancy and earth mysteries books of John Michell, Paul Devereux and others. The details may vary from writer to writer, but the concepts remain similar.

Interestingly, many Christian churches are sited and built on good geomantic principles. Often they are located over the places where our pre-Christian ancestors worshiped their gods. The earth energies at these places were recognised as being ideal places to continue worshipping the gods, no matter what the people's beliefs and doctrines.

Similar respect for the universal energies and man-made structures can be seen in the Egyptian Pyramids, at Delphi and in various structures and mounds built in North and South America.

**SUMMARY**

Many Western educated people appear to have lost that intuitive feel for the earth and its energies which our ancestors took for granted. Our modern life style has increased the drift away from using these intuitive feelings by emphasising the material, tangible world. However, it appears there is a conscious shift taking place to rediscover these ancient and traditional methods and adapt them to our modern lifestyles. An interpretation of these intuitive feelings about places is possible through a knowledge of feng shui and geomancy.

We are also slowly starting to accept that ancient structures like Stonehenge are more than just piles of rocks. They have been constructed with incredible accuracy. The common theme is that they represent some form of the "stars" or heaven on earth, that they are places of high earth energies, and that they attracted a form of age-old worship related to the cyclic changes of seasons.

A knowledge of the key concepts of feng shui and geomancy can help to develop an understanding of the world around us as well as enhancing your current home or business environment.

# 2

# *Elements of Geomancy*

Peoples' relationship with the built and natural environment is affected by a number of elements which can be broadly grouped under the term geomancy. The elements of geomancy include feng shui, electromagnetic energies, natural earth energies, building materials, building systems and design, and history. No one element stands completely alone, however while the concepts of feng shui form the focus of this book the impact of the other elements should be acknowledged. The elements of geomancy in our modern world are summarised in the following paragraphs to form an overview of the subject.

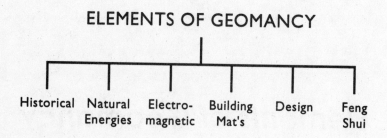

*Figure 2.1 Elements of geomancy*

## FENG SHUI

Feng shui is one of the more complex and sophisticated forms of geomancy. The underlying premise of feng shui is that the design, layout and location of places where you live or work influence the health, wealth, career, relationship and fame aspects of your life. When you make even a few elementary alterations based on feng shui concepts, positive "coincidences" sometimes happen. It is based on the flow of chi or energy in the external environment and within a place.

## NATURAL EARTH ENERGIES

Recent studies have confirmed that the respect ancient people had for the land, in whatever form, was well founded. Many doctors in Europe have noticed a correlation between disease in people, and places where natural earth energies are out of balance. (see Appendix C) These earth energies are called various names from "harmful earth rays" to "geopathic stress" to "negative earth energies". Found by dowsing or divination techniques, they are thought to be a trigger for many diseases, as they appear to unsettle people's energetic and physical bodies by reducing the immune system's ability to fight disease.

They are generally recognised as energies created at the earth's surface by geological faults, underground water streams and geomagnetic energies. It has been observed that if people spend a lot of time at these places, that is if their bed or desk is over these unbalanced earth energies, they are more likely to be tired, listless or unwell, despite the best attention that modern medicine can provide. Often after some corrections to the earth energies, the people begin to recover their health.

The adjustment of these energies should not be seen as the cure for any of the diseases, however it is certainly a subject worth investigating, in conjunction with traditional and modern medical practices to resolve the more puzzling health problems in some people. Often the location of the home is a factor in why people are continually sick.

## ELECTROMAGNETIC ENERGIES

Recent studies have shown a link between the presence of electromagnetic fields in our homes or offices and the occurrence of disease. (see Appendix B) This invisible twentieth century energy appears to affect people in similar ways to the natural earth energies. The scientific community is still arguing about the techniques used in some studies, but the evidence is mounting that electromagnetic energy could be the next "asbestos" issue in homes and business places.

Experience from consultations, indicates that a link exists between electromagnetic fields and insomnia at the very least. Other studies have shown possible links to increased incidence of leukemia, cancer, suicide and other diseases.

## BUILDING MATERIALS, BUILDING SYSTEMS AND DESIGN

Since the Industrial Revolution, more and more sophisticated forms of building materials have been used which have sometimes impacted adversely on our health. Our senses are continually being bombarded by the emissions of modern building materials in our environment.We only need to think of the use of asbestos, oil-based paints and the recent use of various plastics or glues, which continue to emit harmful gases for up to eighteen months after their first use.

Building systems for heating and cooling have also affected the lives of many people in various buildings. The concept of the sick building syndrome is always worth considering in any study of geomancy.

We should be careful in the selection and application of building materials, building systems and their design applications.

## HISTORICAL

Any study of feng shui and geomancy should consider the historical use of the built and natural environment. Our ancestors traditional ways of adapting to their environment and in particular their respect for the earth energies and the chi of the environment, offers clues on how we can best blend modern and ancient practices to our advantage.

**SUMMARY**

There are many elements of geomancy that compliment a study of feng shui. It is important to consider all these aspects of geomancy in the design and layout of both our internal and external environment.

# 3

# *Feng Shui Defined*

Traditionally many people have thought of feng shui as a science of observation.

Our modern understanding of scientific observation comes from drawing rules based on the observation of natural phenomena like astronomy or reactions in chemical experiments. Modern science has endeavoured to give structure to the knowledge gained from observation and to standardise the methods for doing this. However, in recent years we have seen a growing interest in the traditional and non-European understandings of knowledge, which have been based on experiment, observation and refinement over thousands of years.

The idea of feng shui being a science has developed because experimentation is exactly what people do to the environment of their homes and workplaces. People often adjust and change their homes and offices, with new furnishings, new paint colours, by renovating or by moving. So they are trying a new mix of environment to see if they feel more comfortable than before, just like the scientists and their chemicals.

People have expectations that the change will make them feel better, but sometimes it doesn't. Continually changing things in a place may just leave the person feeling uneasy and restless. An understanding of feng shui offers a more systematic or scientific way the desire for change can be applied.

## DEFINING GEOMANCY

In chapter one feng shui was referred to as chinese geomancy and geomancy was defined as "divination or messages from the earth" based on a dictionary definition. However geomancy and feng shui are more than this.

The dictionary definition can be expanded to describe geomancy as a science or system to adjust universal energies or chi to allow human habitats to then be in balance and harmony with the visible and invisible world. The words of the expanded definition allow a greater understanding of where and why it can be applied in our modern world.

## UNIVERSAL ENERGY OR CHI

Many ancient cultures believed that a universal energy or life force (known variously as Chi or Qi or Prana or Mana or Ki) permeates everything. The whole basis of their belief systems was that this universal energy or life force is vital for human existence, in addition to the energy of sunlight, air and water.

In her book *Feng Shui* (p21), Sarah Rossbach defines the sometimes difficult to grasp concept of chi as:-

*"Chi is the vital force that breathes life into the animals and vegetation, inflates the earth to form mountains, and carries water through the earth's ducts........Without chi, trees will not blossom, rivers will not flow, man will not be".*

As Western and Eastern cultures are now blending their knowledge more than ever before, it is becoming easier for the modern western mind to accept this concept of universal energy or life force. We see the use of this concept being applied in the work of acupuncturists, kinesiologists, reiki channels, vibrational healers, sometimes doctors, and feng shui practitioners.

The more you apply feng shui, the more you will start to sense the chi flow in a place. In our modern world the concept of chi could be compared with electricity, radio waves or mobile telephone energies. We can't see them, but they are all around us and with the flick of a switch these invisible energies create sound or reactions of appliances. All of these reactions are connected to the concept of energy in our environment.

Science can no longer dismiss the concept of our energetic body existing outside our physical bodies, as the former can now be photographed and analysed by Kirlian photographs. Often disease can be seen in the auric body before it shows in the physical body.

Basically, everything in the world is energy or chi and it is our perception of that energy ie. whether something is solid, liquid or gas, or chi which depends our belief system.

Our Western educators have done a good job of teaching us the scientific way of appraising the world, but it is not difficult, based on our growing experiences of other forms of energy, to have a much wider understanding of energy as per Ancient and Eastern philosophies.

Some examples of the various chi energies that affect us can be summarised in the figure opposite.

The figure lists the many heaven and earth chi forces that affect people. Human chi is located between heaven's chi and earth's chi. We are the meat in the energetic sandwich, reacting in many ways to various combinations of these forces.

---

Figure 3.1 has been adapted and modified from a concept presented by Howard Choy to a seminar at The Institute of Architects, Sydney, May 1994.

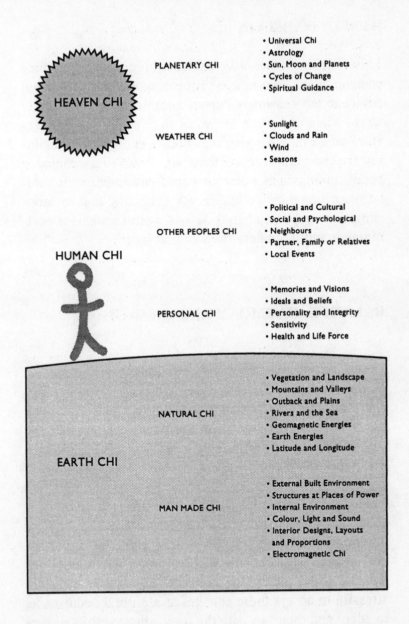

**HEAVEN CHI**

PLANETARY CHI
- Universal Chi
- Astrology
- Sun, Moon and Planets
- Cycles of Change
- Spiritual Guidance

WEATHER CHI
- Sunlight
- Clouds and Rain
- Wind
- Seasons

**HUMAN CHI**

OTHER PEOPLES CHI
- Political and Cultural
- Social and Psychological
- Neighbours
- Partner, Family or Relatives
- Local Events

PERSONAL CHI
- Memories and Visions
- Ideals and Beliefs
- Personality and Integrity
- Sensitivity
- Health and Life Force

**EARTH CHI**

NATURAL CHI
- Vegetation and Landscape
- Mountains and Valleys
- Outback and Plains
- Rivers and the Sea
- Geomagnetic Energies
- Earth Energies
- Latitude and Longitude

MAN MADE CHI
- External Built Environment
- Structures at Places of Power
- Internal Environment
- Colour, Light and Sound
- Interior Designs, Layouts and Proportions
- Electromagnetic Chi

*Figure 3.1   Elements of Chi*

## HUMAN HABITATS

This is just another way of describing your immediate environment - your home, office or workplace. The word environment has many "green" implications on a larger world scale and these are valid to consider for our survival on earth, but sometimes they seem too overwhelming for individuals to contemplate. Practising geomancy entails taking charge of your micro-environment or habitat, your home or workplace. By balancing and harmonising that space you help yourself, your immediate environment and ultimately the world at large.

## BALANCE, HARMONY AND CHANGE

In the modern Westernised world many external influences are constantly changing and often people respond by changing their homes or businesses in subtle, and sometimes not so subtle ways, trying to achieve balance and harmony to compensate for this.

This inclination to change is not unusual when you consider that the natural world is constantly changing our environment with the seasons. This perpetual universal change affects the balance and harmony of both our bodies and environment. It is more productive and less stressful to accept these changes as a normal occurrence, to adapt and then "go with the flow", than to try and stay fixed or rigid, and attempt to resist these changes and cycles. People who resist change often do so out of a fear of the unknown, and this fear frequently has consequences in the state of their health and "fortune". Our whole existence is often based on these cycles of what The Five Element Theory (See Appendix A) terms growth and decay or expansion and contraction.

Eastern philosophies define the extent of these changes in terms of yin (relatively more passive) and yang (relatively more active) or Taoism (pronounced "daoism") where these philosophies are applied to achieve a balance of yin and yang energies despite any change.

It is important to note the word "relative", as yin and yang are complementary. They are not extreme examples, or conflicts in a "positive and negative" Western sense, such as good and bad. For example, a hot day of 20°C in London (yang) is relative to the average weather conditions in London of say 12°C (yin), but 20°C in London would now become more yin if compared to a summer's day in Singapore with a very yang temperature of 30°C.

The concept of relative yin and yang is important when considering the feng shui balance of a home or business. For example if a home or business is full of activity (more yang) and needs calming down, then the application and types of corrections needed for this place may be different from somewhere which is more peaceful and serene (more yin), but lacks the activity needed to allow the chi to flow smoothly throughout it. Feng shui can help to create a more balanced environment to achieve more harmony and equilibrium in either situation.

## INVISIBLE AND VISIBLE

Many invisible energies affect our lives in terms of the balance and harmony of our larger visible environment. We feel the changes in the weather bought on by the change in seasons, even though we cannot see the energy that causes the change. What we see is visible changes caused by invisible forces. The movement of the tides by the moon is another example of the impact of the invisible on the visible world.

Our visible world is very real to us. We understand the impact that the colour, size and shape of a room or building can have on us. If you walk into a room which is painted red your reaction is totally different from your response to a white room. The visible and the invisible can be represented in a number of ways, such as the idea of an iceberg where the visible part above the water is only a small part of the total mass. The visible part cannot exist without the huge invisible section under the water.

Our world is very similar in that the invisible can sometimes have a larger impact on us. We can't see sound, frequency or vibration, electricity or electromagnetic fields, wind or energy or atoms, but they unquestionably are part of our everyday life. In the visible world the built environment, natural topography such as rivers, mountains and the sea, continually affect our feelings for a place. The invisible is dependent on the visible and vice versa.

Feng shui principles expand the concept of the invisible affecting our lives. In feng shui terms the shape and location of rooms and buildings can have a profound affect on

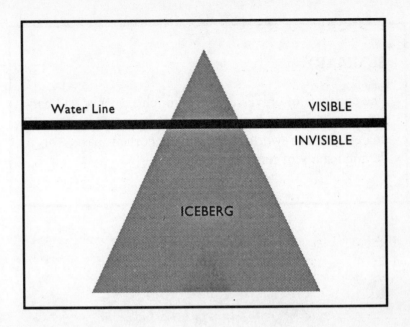

*Figure 3.2  Invisible vs Visible*

the occupants. For example, if you have your bathroom in the wealth corner of your house, then your money is likely to be flushed away. It would be easy to dismiss this and many other feng shui ideas as superstition except that too many peoples' eyes light up with recognition that their toilet is in the wealth corner of their home or business and they are having wealth, abundance or financial troubles. When those people later make feng shui corrections and see changes in their wealth or abundance the notion of superstition quickly disappears. This is not to say that they go out and win the lottery immediately after making the corrections, but rather that they restore an energetic balance in their home or office and this subsequently creates more harmony and prosperity in their lives.

**SUMMARY**

The concepts of universal energy or chi, balance and harmony, invisible and visible energy and the cycles of change in our world form an important basis for a detailed study of feng shui

# 4

# *Feng Shui and the External Environment*

Feng shui principles have developed from Fu Hsi's Early Lo Map and the observation of various elements of the external environment, which were used to determine the most auspicious place to bury a family's ancestors. This chapter will outline how these external influences can be developed to apply to the modern world.

However it is firstly important to understand that there are two schools of feng shui - the classical school and the intuitive school.

# THE CLASSICAL SCHOOL OF FENG SHUI

This is the ancient style of feng shui, based on the use of a geomancer's compass or luopan. The luopan consists of many concentric rings which reflect such features as : the five elements of nature : the eight primary trigrams : directions of the compass and Nine Star Ki information.

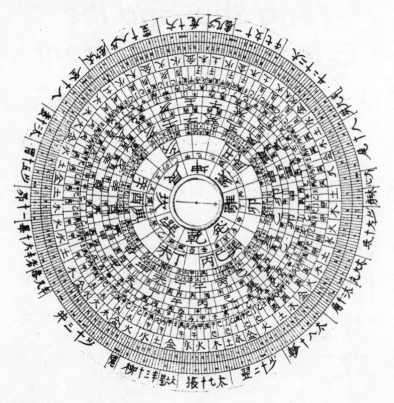

*Figure 4.1 Luopan*

To become a classical feng shui master requires many years of practice and apprenticeship in Asian countries where a cultural understanding would be conveyed from an early age. It would be almost impossible for a Western educated person to ever become a feng shui master in the classical school. They are more likely to be feng shui consultants who base their work on the intuitive application of the principles. This is not to say that their application of the principles is any better or worse, but simply that they apply them with a different cultural understanding. They can be just as successful in the Western world where they can apply the principles within a culture they understand.

## THE INTUITIVE SCHOOL OF FENG SHUI

The study of other cultures by Western educated people, and information provided by the many people of Asian heritage who now live in Western societies, has resulted in an intuitive school of feng shui. This method has developed from a greater understanding throughout the world of Eastern philosophies and a wider acceptance of the validity of non-European approaches to life. The approach of this school is to combine the age-old principles of feng shui with intuition, common sense and a cultural understanding of the society where it is to be applied, so that the best of both worlds can be achieved. Feng shui within the intuitive school involves observation, intuition and feeling, based on the basic rules that have been formulated over thousands of years of observation. This book is based on the principles of the intuitive approach to feng shui.

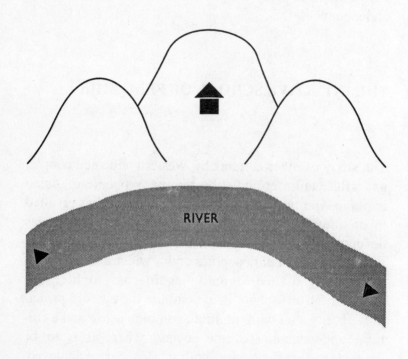

*Figure 4.2   Classic Diagram of External Landscape*

## THE EXTERNAL ENVIRONMENT

Whichever system is used, the first thing to observe is the influence of the larger scale external environment on a place and then to consider the source and amount of chi flow on the land around the place you are assessing. Look at the influences of rivers, roads, mountains, trees, buildings, etc. around the home or business being assessed. Look particularly for those things which will affect the chi flow around, toward or away from the place and the source of chi. When looking for the source of chi observe any blockages or over-exposures.

From the diagram opposite it can be seen that traditionally the most auspicious place to site your home or business is half-way up a mountain with the protective "arms" of mountains embracing each side, just like the shape of a big old fashioned arm chair, and with a gentle flowing river across the face of the opening of the mountains. This way the home is protected at the rear and sides and it enjoys a gentle flow of chi coming around your place from the "wind". The "water" container of chi is provided within the sides of the mountains.

Very few of us have the opportunity to live in surroundings like this, however we can transfer the general principle back to the place where we live or work. The general features of the places where we live need to be considered in terms of the natural and man-made landscape around us.

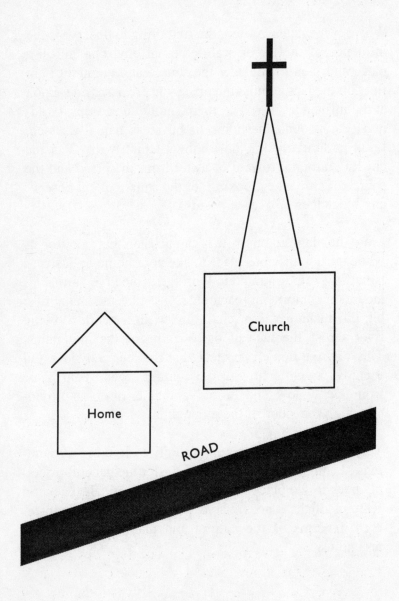

*Figure 4.3   Church Spire and Home*

## EXTERNAL STRUCTURES

Firstly the mountains in the classic diagram of the external landscape (figure 4.2) may be replaced by trees or other buildings in your general locality. So look and assess the main features around your place. Do they help protect your back and sides or do they overpower you? It is a fine balance which can only be decided by your assessment of the proportions. Again you don't want extreme examples of buildings, mountains or trees (too much yang energy) right on top of your home or office.

By standing at the front of your building and looking at either side and at the rear, observe the proportions of the environment around you. If they are too large (too yang) the energy of these features may need to be modified, or if you are too exposed without much protection (too yin) you may need to provide that protection.

For example, if there is a church with a tall spire next door to your home as indicated in Figure 4.3, the church's energy will be overpowering. You may need to break that energy by planting tall trees along the boundary between your home and the church.

Other solutions or cures based on the concepts of the nine basic cures (chapter six) may even be applicable in certain circumstances. Please remember: no matter what the solution, it should feel appropriate to your cultural, social and environmental situation. The first step in your feng shui assessment of any place is to consider the impact of the surrounding man-made structures and the natural landscape.

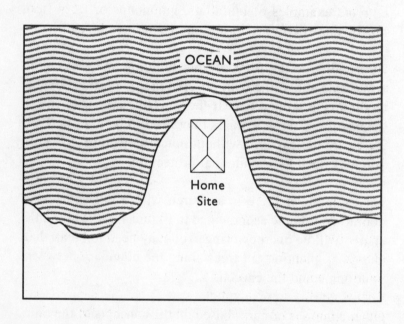

*Figure 4.4 Home on Point near Ocean*

## SOURCES OF CHI

The other aspect of the external environment influencing your place is the source of chi or the "river of chi" seen in the classic diagram of the external landscape (figure 4.2).

### The Ocean or Sea

If your home is located near the ocean, then is it too exposed? The house on the peninsula illustrated opposite is getting too much chi from the ocean. There is a need to correct this yang situation with trees or similar barriers around the house to reduce its exposure without affecting its often magnificent view. The amount and size of these trees will depend on the amount of balancing of energy the people now living in this house require.

Everyone's need of chi from their environment will vary according to their lifestyle and what is happening in their lives. This is a fundamental premise of intuitive feng shui. Firstly to understand what you feel is out of balance in your life, analyse where this is reflected in your environment and then make the appropriate adjustments. Remember the adjustments for one home or business in a given situation may be totally inappropriate for another home or business in the same place.

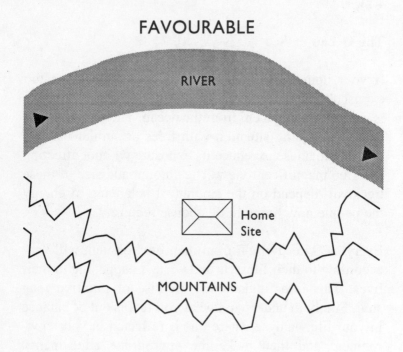

*Figure 4.5 Favourable Home Site near River*

## A River

Another possible source of chi to consider is that of an inland river or stream. Figures 4.5 and 4.6 illustrate possible examples of river flow and the favourable or unfavourable location of home sites. The unfavourable location has too much chi directed at it.

## UNFAVOURABLE

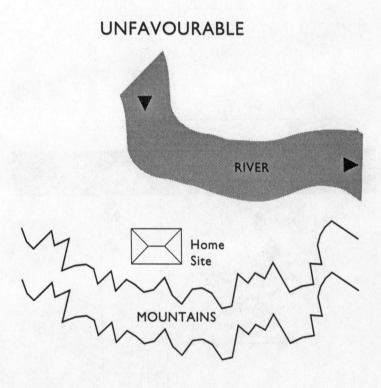

*Figure 4.6 Unfavourable Home Site near River*

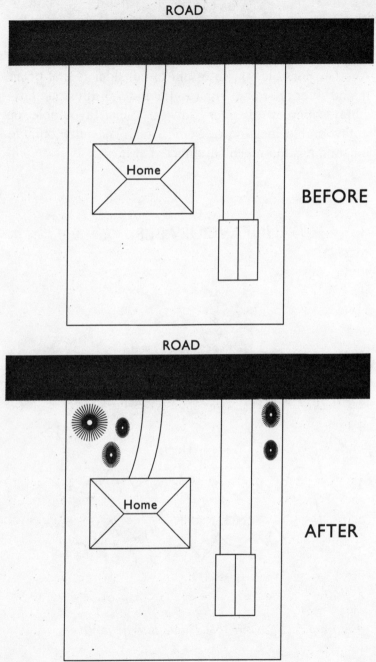

Figure 4.7  *Homes In Street*

## Roads

Many homes are not near the ocean or rivers, but are nearly always near roads which carry traffic and movement with them. Here we start to see how the principles are applied symbolically. The movement of traffic on the road is symbolic of the flow of water in a river.

For example, the chi will often pass by the house or land in a suburban street, if there is no attempt to capture chi with some trees or shrubs along our boundaries like the mountains in the classic diagram. Most people do this intuitively anyway, but it is always a good reminder to start with the basics. Some chi needs to be gathered, otherwise opportunities will continually pass by you and your house.

The intensity of the chi movement and the size of the trees or shrubs will vary depending on the rate of flow of the traffic. A main road potentially has more chi flow than a quiet suburban street and would require different corrections.

Another factor in chi flow is whether the road passes straight across the front of the property, curves gently across the property or whether it is aimed directly at the front door.

The "worst" location is at the end "T" intersection where a home is exposed to too much chi (also known as sha chi). Just as too little chi was a problem for the house illustrated Figure 4.7 - Before, so is too much chi. In particular when that chi is coming in a straight line. It is as if everyone walking or driving towards your place has

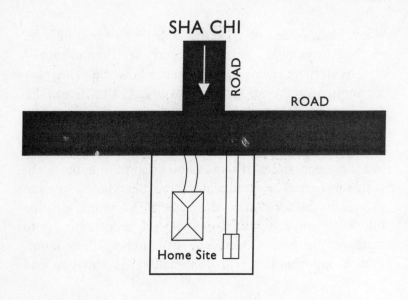

*Figure 4.8 Home Located at "T" Intersection*

you in their sights and is sending their energy, good or bad, towards you. If you do not deflect or slow down that energy, then your house or business will have too much chi and it will be out of balance. A similar situation is found at the end of cul-de- sacs as indicated in Figure 4.8.

You can correct these arrows of chi using some of the principles of the Nine Basic Cures discussed in chapter six such as fountains, windchimes, mirrors, trees or shrubs or similar correction that slows down and "curves" the arrow of chi.

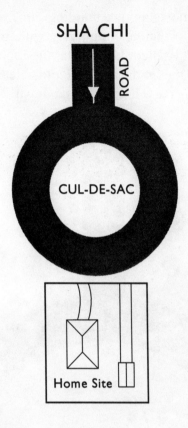

*Figure 4.9 Home located at the end of a Cul-de Sac*

It is interesting to note that objects in the natural landscape are made up of curves and not straight lines just as
the flow of chi within a place is encouraged to move in
curves not straight lines. The application of this principle
is seen in successful shopping centres which overcome
these arrows of chi, by stepping shopfronts in and out to
create "curves of movement" and interesting sight lines,
rather than shops forming long straight corridors.

Some of the most famous buildings in the world have used feng shui principles intuitively without even knowing that this art existed. Looking at the fountain between The Mall and Buckingham Palace, it is clear how the chi from the mall is curved and slowed down.

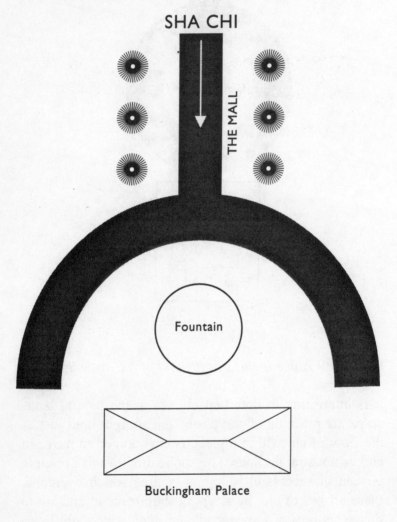

*Figure 4.10 The Mall and Buckingham Palace*

Another example of sha chi can be found in homes where a long front garden path leads directly to the front door. The chi needs to be slowed down, either by curving the front footpath or by placing a correction or cure along the path.

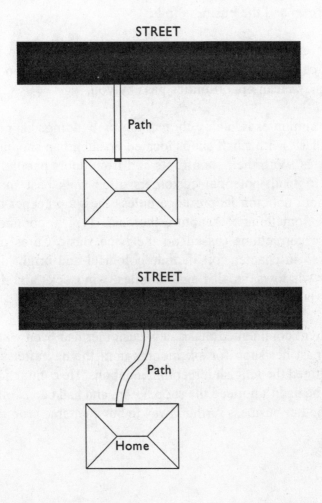

*Figure 4.11 Front Garden Path*

An extension to these ideas often occurs in business. Businesses located at the end of T-junctions often have a high turnover of proprietors and are unsuccessful. Again this is because they have too much chi within their building, causing their customers to feel uncomfortable. They often stop going to the shop, consequently turnover declines and the business fails.

It is important to consider your location relative to the source of chi, too much chi may be unsettling and too little may mean opportunities pass by you.

A common example of chi passing by buildings happens regularly with small shops located on suburban shopping centres. With their shopfronts and front doors parallel to the footpath potential customers often walk past shops without noticing its presence unless the shop keeper has done something to "capture the chi". Typical common-sense corrections (based on the Nine Basic Cures discussed in chapter six) include colourful and bright display windows, small flags, mobiles, windsocks and display boards which are changed regularly.

A client commented that a new customer had been walking past her shop for six months until the day after she instituted the feng shui recommendations. He commented that he hadn't noticed the shop before and had been going to another business further away to buy the same product!

**SUMMARY**

The external environment is the first place that we observe the influence of the natural and man-made landscape around us. It is the first place to adjust the chi flow and containment, before looking at the internal environment of any place.

Feng shui concentrates on achieving a harmonious chi flow in and around a place. Corrections or cures can be applied to modify that flow to bring any place into balance. In applying any of the concepts, it is important to remember that the principles of feng shui are very symbolic, and while they were derived more than two thousand years ago, they can still be applied to our homes or businesses today, if you use your intuition and common sense.

**Exercise**

Go outside the building you are in now and while looking from the front, observe the local external influences, which may be affecting the chi flow in and around that place. What corrections are needed to modify this chi? It may not be obvious at first, however as you travel each day start to look at the influence the external environment has on various buildings and the feeling it creates for you. The more you observe the world around you the more you will come to understand how feng shui works in the external environment.

# 5

# *Shape & Feng Shui*

## THE ROLE OF THE BAGUA

Once the external aspects of the larger environment are understood and corrected, the next factor to consider is the external shape of a home or business. The energetic balance or imbalance caused by the external shape of a place is defined in feng shui in terms of the "bagua".

The bagua (or pakua) developed from the Early Lo Map (Figure 1.2) formulated by the observations of Fu Hsi. Around 1200 BC in the Chou Dynasty, King Wen and the Duke of Chou made some changes to the early Lo Map. Although they believed that Fu Hsi had a great theory, the balance of the eight trigrams didn't allow for any movement or cycles of energy as they were perfectly balanced with corresponding trigrams opposite each other on the map. They recognised that movement and cycles is an essential part of the earth's natural flow. They subsequently altered the Early Lo Map to the Later Lo Map, as indicated below.

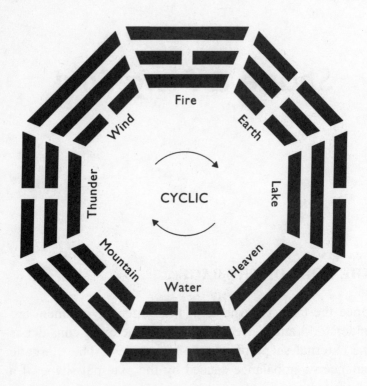

*Figure 5.1 Later Lo Map*

They made some very shrewd changes to introduce this movement without dramatically altering the original basis of the Lo Map. They placed the trigrams for Fire and Water directly opposite each other, Heaven and Earth one apart on the same side, Wind and Thunder next to each other on the same side, and Mountain and Lake two places apart, and on different sides. They gained movement but allowed some balance in the polarity of the Lo

Map. This map is called the Later Lo Map. The bagua was developed from this Later Lo Map.

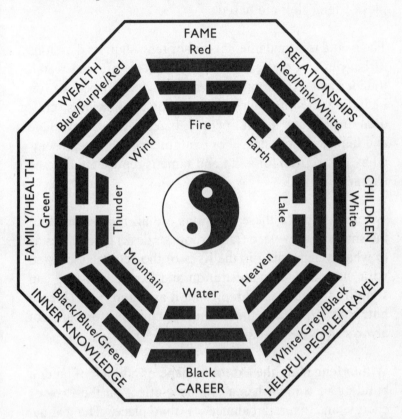

*Figure 5.2 Bagua*

The bagua is again eight trigrams but this time a ninth element in the centre is displayed in the form of the yin/yang symbol of balance and is referred to as the tai chi. It is interesting to note that the layout of the trigrams is reversed between the later lo map and the bagua. It is as if the trigrams for the lo map are read from the centre looking out to the universe, whereas for the bagua we are focussing our energies from the outside back to the centre or tai chi. The tai chi represents balance and harmony in the centre of the bagua on which many of the principles of feng shui are based.

The bagua is a fundamental tool of feng shui. Its divisions of heaven and earth, mountain and lake, fire and water, thunder and wind represent virtually every aspect of life including wealth, fame, marriage or relationships, children or projects, helpful people, career, inner knowledge and family or ancestors. For example wealth is represented by the trigram for wind and fame is represented by the trigram for fire.

Within any place these divisions are all represented and the shape of any place (land, room or desk) gives clues as to what is happening in the lives of the people associated with that place. For illustration and explanation, we can simplify the bagua and represent it as Figure 5.3. (Please note that in practice the "Nine" square divisions are not always square or equally proportioned.)

Within feng shui, the external shape of a block of land, a building or a room has a dramatic effect on the flow of energy and overall balance of that place. The bagua, superimposed over the land, building or room highlights aspects of peoples lives which can be represented by the missing corners in a plan.

A corner or section missing causes an energetic imbalance and may indicate career, relationship, fame, family, wealth, helpful people or inner knowledge problems for the inhabitants. This is not to say that we all should live in square homes, but rather if things are out of balance, we can take steps to correct that imbalance.

| | | |
|---|---|---|
| WEALTH | FAME | RELATIONSHIPS |
| FAMILY/ HEALTH | TAI CHI | CREATIVE/ CHILDREN/ PROJECTS |
| INNER KNOWLEDGE/ INTUITION | CAREER | HELPFUL PEOPLE/ TRAVEL |

FRONT DOOR THIS SIDE

*Figure 5.3 Practical Bagua*

Before looking at the application of the bagua in more detail, some of the basic concepts that are important to its interpretation will be explained. They are firstly the definition of the "front door" which determines the direction in which the bagua is applied, the shape of a place and finally negative space or projections where sections of the bagua are over or under represented.

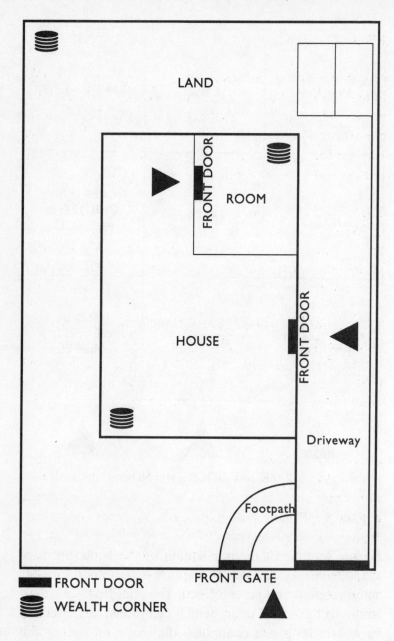

*Figure 5.4  Front door and wealth corners*

# FRONT DOOR

The front door of the land, home, office or room determines the direction in which the bagua is applied to a place. In feng shui the front door is seen as the source of chi of that place, just as our mouths are seen as the doorway for the chi for our bodies. The front door forms the anchor point for the application of the bagua.

The front door of most places is reasonably obvious from a physical viewpoint, but remember we are dealing with the invisible world of energy in the application of these principles and we are actually looking for the energetic front door!

The traditional and classic definition of front door is based on the door where someone coming to your place for the first time would knock. For example a first time visitor or someone delivering a parcel would come to your "front door". This applies even if 99% of all other people all come to your back door.

In an apartment block or office, the front door to your place is the front door of your apartment or office. If you were applying feng shui to the entire building, you would use the front door to the building. The front door then applies to whatever space you are balancing. If you are balancing a block of land, apply the bagua to the land shape based on the front door to the land. If you are balancing a house, apply it to the house shape, based on the front door of the house. If you are balancing a room, apply it to the room shape based on the front door of the room. Figure 5.4 shows these different applications of

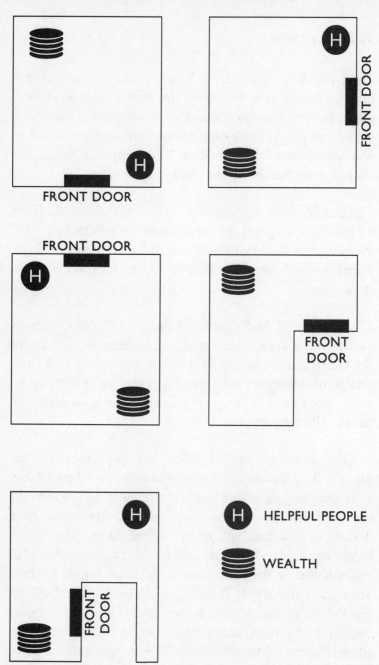

*Figure 5.5 Front door examples*

front door and the wealth corner for each element.

Figure 5.5 gives further examples of the relationship between bagua and front door. The front door is always projected to the external edge of the shape of a bagua. It will always be in or projected through the "Inner Knowledge", "Career" or "Helpful People" sections.

## INTUITION CAN BREAK THE RULES

The definition of front door may not always be as simple as the traditional definition above. Some houses have multiple doors which could be the front door to the house, depending on the interpretation of the classical definition or the "back" door could be the energetic front door.

It is important not to get completely caught up in the traditional rules, as sometimes they don't provide the answers for your particular situation. Go back to basics and think about what you are trying to do - balance the chi or energy of a place. To achieve this decisions should be based on how our bodies are affected energetically by the application of these rules. Some people have developed their intuitive skills to a point where they just know energetically what needs balancing in a place and where the energetic front door is located. Unfortunately most of us don't have that sensitivity (yet).

However, most people can use a dowsing rod or pendulum, or be taught to use them in a very short period of

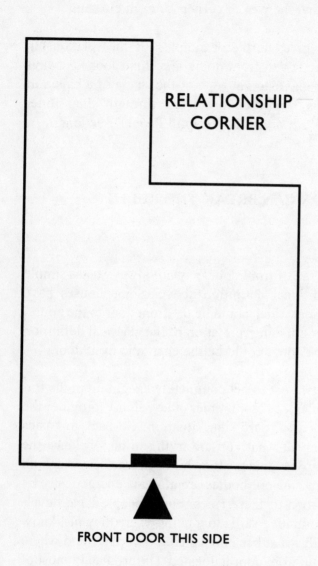

*Figure 5.6  Relationship house shape*

time. (See appendix D). By using a pendulum or dowsing rod, it is possible to respond to the energetic effect on people of a particular place. So if you are unsure of which is your energetic front door, you can always use these devices to ask the question: "Where is my energetic front door?" If you use a rod, then the rod will point to the "energetic front door." If you are using a pendulum, you might ask: "Is this door the energetic front door to this house or room?"

Establishing the front door is usually quite obvious, but every so often you need the extra help of the dowsing rod or pendulum. Once the front door is established for the place you are balancing, you can then layout the bagua and consider the impact of the shape of a place in terms of feng shui.

## WHAT SHAPE?

People don't all live in square houses with the bagua nicely balanced and even if they did, other factors may be throwing the chi out of kilter. The majority of people live in apartments or homes, or work in places that are not square in external shape. So in terms of the bagua they have a "piece" missing. The best way to explain the concept of shape and the bagua is to consider a home of the shape indicated in figure 5.6.

According to the rules of feng shui people who live or work in places shaped like this tend to have relationship problems with their partners, clients or children. These problems may not start from day one of living in that place, but the unbalanced energy of the place will eventually begin to affect those people's lives. So apartments

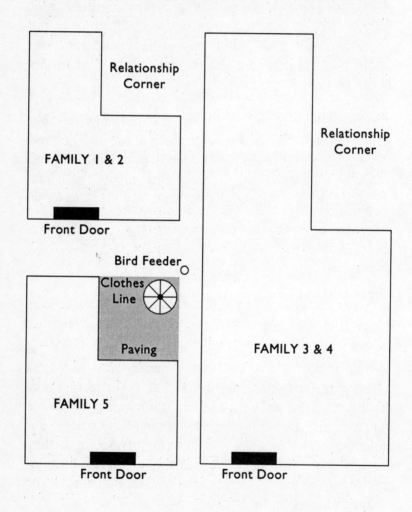

*Figure 5.7 Relationship Homes of Five Families*

and houses shaped like this tend to house single people, separated people or people who have had difficulties in establishing satisfactory relationships.

To illustrate this point, five houses assessed in the past twelve months had the "relationship/marriage" corner missing (when viewed from the front door, the top right-hand corner is missing and not balanced in any way see the diagram of the bagua above and the house outlined below). Four of the families involved were in the middle of separation and divorce proceedings and had made no corrections to this missing corner, but the fifth family were as happy as ever, having intuitively balanced the missing corner with a defined paving layout, a bird feeder and clothes line. These corrections all generate chi and balance the bagua. Any correction or cure that provides movement can be used to help energise the missing corners. (The "Nine Basic Cures" or energy corrections will be discussed in the next chapter).

The representations of corners missing can apply equally to most other shapes, but any adjustments to the shape of a place should only occur if that is what the occupants want balanced in their lives. There is no need to correct the relationship corner, if someone is perfectly happy with their life as a single person at that point in time.

As a general guideline the shape is generally thought to be your legal boundaries for blocks of land, apartments or offices. However with home shapes some other questions are often raised regarding pergolas, garages, verandas and carports. Firstly again trust your intuition as to what feels like the shape that energetically represents your home. One way to establish the shape is to imagine that

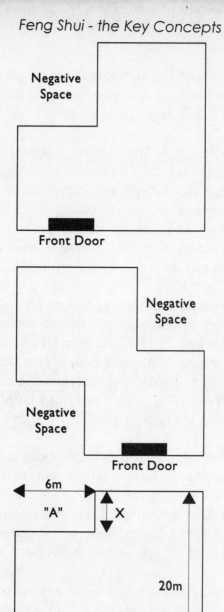

*Figure 5.8  Negative Space*

if you were in a helicopter looking down on your place, what is the roof shape of the habitable rooms. In eighty percent of cases this will establish the shape to be used when applying the bagua. If, however, you have a carport or garage attached to the side of your house, generally this does not form part of this shape, unless the roof line is continuous between the house and carport. This principle also applies in other similar situations. If in doubt try asking questions with a pendulum.

# NEGATIVE SPACE AND PROJECTIONS

Negative space in a place is defined as a part that is missing in a shape, just as the relationship corner was obviously missing in the example above.

However what if the piece missing is only small? How big is small? The illustration opposite shows two clear cut examples of negative space. The third drawing shows a wealth corner (A) possibly missing or relationship and fame projecting, depending on the size of the dimension noted as "X".

While it is not possible to give an exact definition of what is a projection and what is negative space, for illustration the space indicated as "A" would be negative space if the dimension X was greater than about 0.5m in most circumstances. Conversely if it was less than about 0.5m the relationship and fame areas would be seen as a projection. Whereas the negative space indicating something missing in a layout, projection shows an area that may be overemphasised in someone's life based on the bagua.

The above example gives some general guidelines about negative space and projection, but don't ever be afraid to use your intuitive feel about how these principles can be applied to your place.

A classic example of the idea of projection is the oval office is located in the fame section of the "White House".

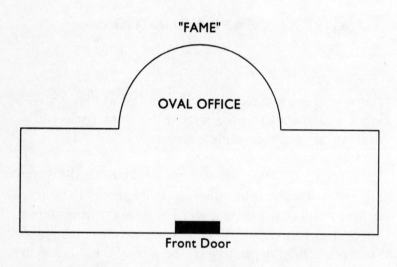

*Figure 5.9 White House*

**SUMMARY**

The feng shui of any place should be assessed going from the larger external environment down to the smallest details in the house or office.

A simple procedure to follow if you are looking at a house would be to firstly look at the external environment influences discussed in chapter four then apply the bagua to the block of land based on the front door to the block of land, then apply another bagua to the shape of your house based on the front door of the house; then apply the bagua to each room in the house, based on the front door to each room. Finally look at some of the other energetic concepts discussed in chapter 8. The process of refining and observing the overall energy balance of a place is ongoing.

**Exercise**

Sketch the shape of your home or office and determine if any corners/ sections are missing. Does this reflect what is happening in your life in this place? Or have you intuitively generated chi in the missing sections?

# 6

# Nine Basic Cures

If after reading the previous chapters you realise that your place is out of balance or needs the flow of chi modified, then feng shui provides what are termed the "Nine Basic Cures" or energy corrections that can be applied to your home or business. At this stage don't worry if the cures are not appropriate to the decor of your home or work, just remember that it is the symbolic application of these cures that is important.

The basic purpose of the cures is to either generate additional chi, slow down chi directed in a straight line, anchor chi or capture chi. Most of the cures use some form of energy, be it light, sound, wind, water or combination of these energies.

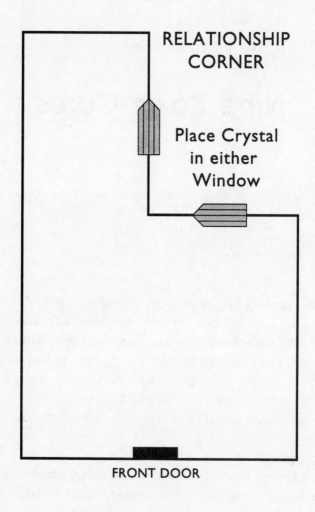

RELATIONSHIP
CORNER

Place Crystal
in either
Window

FRONT DOOR

*Figure 6.1  Relationship Corner Corrected with a Crystal*

# 1. BRIGHT OBJECTS

## Crystals

Classic feng shui crystals are small spherical lead glass crystals, not the naturally occurring rose quartz or citrine type crystals. They generate chi by drawing in the external light energy and often create rainbows of colour on the walls of the room where they are used. Using the relationship example from the previous chapter, we could put a crystal in the window as shown below, which would draw in the "negative space" of the missing corner.

For those people living in apartments or working in offices with missing "Relationship" corners may think: "How can I do this? I don't have windows on this elevation, and I can't go into the neighbours' place to square off the corner that's missing." This is where the next feng shui cure, mirrors can be used.

## Mirrors

Mirrors probably the most common form of cure used in feng shui, are used to bring in the chi when negative space makes a shape out of balance. In our "relationship" example above, energy can be drawn into the missing

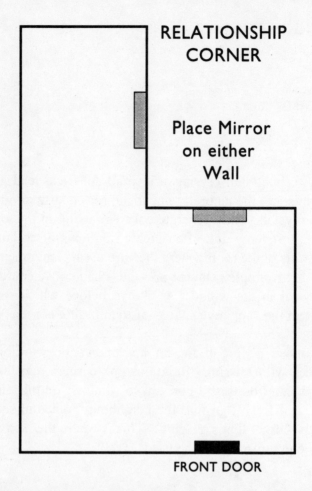

*Figure 6.2   Relationship Corner Corrected with a Mirror*

relationship corner by placing mirrors on the wall in either place shown below.

This use of mirrors will work well in any situation where they are appropriate to the decor. But what if large mirrors are inappropriate to the decor? Or what if you have fixed furniture all along both those walls? What do you do? Again remember the energetic basis of feng shui. The symbolism and intent in any corrections you make are always worth respecting and understanding. It may be possible to symbolically use small mirrors, tucked behind furniture or paintings and still achieve the same result. If this is your only option, then try the smaller mirrors and see if your life comes more into balance in the next few months. If not, other aspects of your layout may need reviewing. Mirrors can also be used to reflect in the chi from outside.

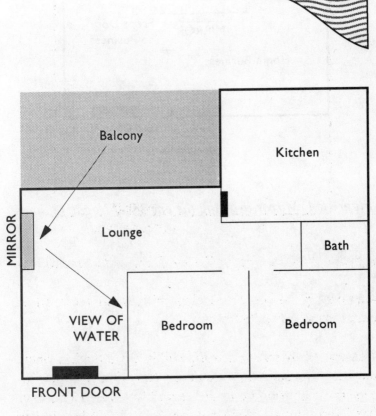

*Figure 6.3  Mirror reflecting outside chi*

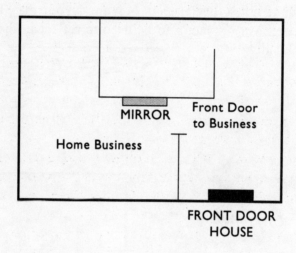

*Figure 6.4  Mirror drawing the energy of Negative Space*

The relationship examples used above have been based on the idea of balancing the overall shape of a house, but the same principles apply to rooms within a home. An example within a home that helps to clarify the concept of corners missing and the use of a mirror to draw in the energy of that negative space is illustrated below.

A small business operates within the lounge/dining area of a typical suburban house shown opposite. The proprietor was finding it difficult to get people to help in the business. So the shape of the space the business operated from was assessed, and "coincidentally" it was found that the "Helpful People" corner was completely missing. With the aid of a mirror on the wall, helpful people were found almost instantaneously. At an open day for the business one week later the proprietor had several offers of help from various people, whereas at every other open day she had struggled to look after her clients by herself.

Mirrors are more than just reflective cures for negative space, their power and use will be discussed further in the next chapter.

**Lights**

Similarly, electrical lighting can also generate chi in corners that need correcting.

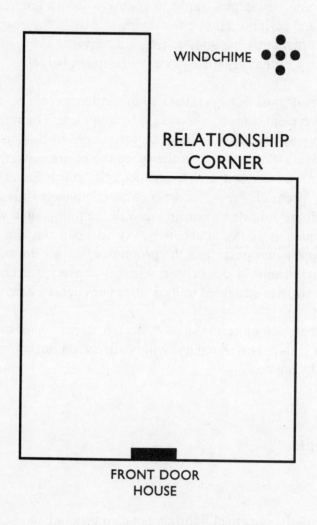

*Figure 6.5 Relationship Corner Corrected with a Windchime*

## 2. SOUNDS

The movement and sound, of windchimes and bells can also be used to generate chi. In our "relationship" example above, the house could have been symbolically squared off using a windchime or bell placed in the corner as illustrated in figure 6.5.

Another client who also worked from home, found that after a windchime was placed in the wealth corner of her consulting room, the next client gave her a $20 tip. She had never received a tip from any client before.

## 3. LIVING OBJECTS

Living objects in the form of plants, flowers and fish in fish tanks generate chi, as well as being appealing decorating objects for any home or business.

### Plants

These can be used indoors or outdoors. In the classic relationship example, a tree could be placed near the corner of the relationship section to symbolically square the house and generate chi.

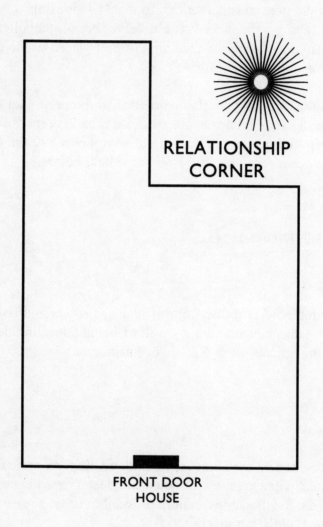

RELATIONSHIP
CORNER

FRONT DOOR
HOUSE

*Figure 6.6  Relationship Corner Corrected with a Tree*

Plants and trees are an important part of any environment. In addition to beautifying our landscape and purifying our air, they can, if placed strategically, generate or capture chi, or deflect and slow down sha chi. The use of plants in our landscape is a very important tool of feng shui.

Indoor plants and flowers tend to lift the chi in any place. They can lift the chi in corners that may be out of balance. Homes and offices that feel good often have lively indoor plants which are pleasing to our eye. Rounded leaf plants are preferred to sharp, spiky-leafed plants.

## Fish Bowls

Used as feng shui corrections, these can be very powerful. The water element is symbolic of being receptive to other forms of energy, and the fish keep moving, and thus generate chi.

In successful Chinese restaurants it is interesting to observe where their fish bowls or tanks are placed. It will often be near the cash register or front door. Money is seen as a form of energy and the fish tank helps to attract cash. Figure 6.7 illustrates a simple example of a typical layout.

The number of fish is also important and you would never see four fish in a fish bowl, as the word four in chinese is very similar to the word for death. Eight is the most

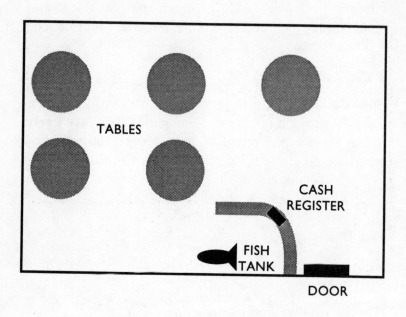

*Figure 6.7 Fish Tank and Cash Register*

powerful number, but most other numbers are acceptable.

Recently, a friend who knows nothing of feng shui built a large fish tank. His business had been quiet and he had some spare time. Intuitively he took the fish tank home and put it in the wealth corner of the house, and also put it in the wealth corner of that room. Within two weeks his business was booming again, and he was forced to work double shifts to keep up with the demand. His business

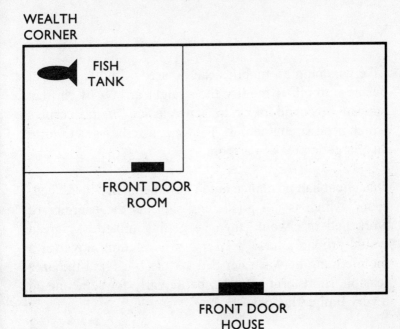

*Figure 6.8  Fish Tank in Wealth Corner*

has continued to flourish as has his fish collection. He now has three tanks in all. A side benefit has been that his children watch less television as they often sit and watch more than two hundred fish swimming around!

## 4. MOVING OBJECTS

Any moving objects like mobiles, fountains and windmills generate chi and often help to slow chi down or modify sha chi.

## Mobiles

Like windchimes, mobiles can be used within a home or business to either modify the straight arrows of chi that happen in corridors or to generate chi in the corners which need strengthening. They can also be used to form an energetic break in a room.

One client had no choice but to have her office in her bedroom, which is not good feng shui, as the energies of work and rest would then be getting mixed. A screen would probably have been the best solution, however a mobile hung between her bed and desk offered the only feasible short term solution, particularly for someone on a very limited budget.

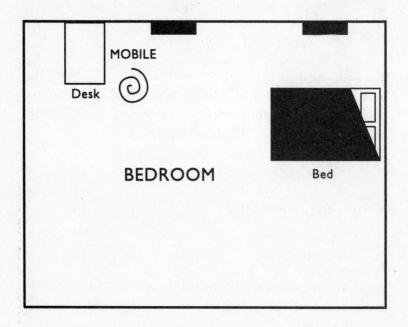

*Figure 6.9   Mobile in Bedroom*

## Fountains

Fountains can be used to generate chi in landscapes, gardens or internal displays. Water is always a good symbol for flowing energy as well as being a good absorber of energy. They can also be used to slow down and divert sha chi as discussed in chapter four.

## Windmills

Windmills or even symbols of windmills can also generate chi.

## 5. HEAVY OBJECTS

The use of stones or statues or any heavy object is seen as a way of anchoring the chi in a particular place on the bagua.

For example, to stabilise a relationship, a heavy object placed in the relationship corner of a bedroom may help. Heavy objects are often found marking the doorway to homes or offices. They are seen as framing the "mouth of chi" or doorway to a place. They may also take on the role of "protectors" if they are lions or dragons, which are often sited at the entrance to the "Chinatown" areas in the major capital cities of the world or to the entrances of restaurants, business premises and homes.

A recent client was having difficulty holding onto good staff in his business. Three large pot plants with solid pots and lots of soil were placed in the relationship corner of his business, and his staff turnover stabilised.

## 6. ELECTRICAL OBJECTS

### Stereos

The sound of radios and stereos generate chi in whatever location they are placed. An important aspect of this cure is the type of music that is being played. For example a local bookshop didn't have many customers until they stopped playing heavy metal music. Another client, a per-fume and cosmetics store, had its best sales when they played Nat King Cole music.

We are very susceptible to the influence of sound. The use and type of music in a home or business needs to be carefully assessed based on the mood you are trying to create.

## Fans

Fans also generate good chi by their movement of air or "wind".

For example, a central ceiling fan often attracts our attention by its movement and chi generation. However, the use of ceiling fans must feel appropriate to the space based on ceiling height. If a ceiling fan is located in a room with high ceilings it is more effective as a feng shui cure than if the fan is in a room with only a standard modern 2.4m (8ft) high ceiling. We feel more comfortable with the ceiling fan being further away from us.

This aspect of geomancy brings in the concepts of proportions and design of rooms based on the ideas of "sacred geometry and architecture".

## 7. SYMBOLIC OBJECTS

In the same way that stereos and radios generate chi with their sound, musical instruments can also be seen to symbolise the generation of chi. A musical instrument doesn't have to be played constantly to achieve this; it is more the intent or symbolism of the object that is important.

A recent client intuitively placed a guitar in the relationship corner of the room, in the relationship corner of her home, soon after a consultation. Within three days of making this change, she met two men at a local jazz

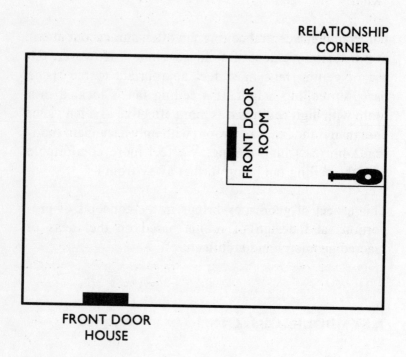

*Figure 6.10 Guitar in Relationship Corner*

nightclub who played the guitar and continued to see one of them after that night.

## 8. COLOURS

The use of colour is a key factor in feng shui as it affects the way we respond to our environment. In particular the colour red is used to generate chi. While too much red in a room can make us feel uncomfortable, the judicious use of red can help add vitality to a business or home. A red front door can help to clearly define the "mouth of chi" if your front door is not clearly defined. Red walls as part of the decorations within a restaurant can help lift the energy enabling diners to eat quickly and thus generating a quicker turnover of people at the tables.

Red ribbon wrapped around, or a thin red stripe painted along the side of a stair banister or handrail will lead people up the stairs. In a two-level restaurant this encourages people to eat on the upper as well as the lower level. Red ribbon wrapped around door handles that clash is thought to lessen arguments in a home or business.

Within the bagua different colours can be applied in different sections. (see Figure 5.2) For example Fame or Fire can be represented by the colour red. So if you are trying to generate more chi in the fame section of your office, you could try making a correction with the colour red, or a fire, or something symbolic of this concept. You could put up a tall sharp mountain poster which represents the shape of fire burning. Similarly, if you are strengthening your career area with a windchime, you might add to the strength of this cure by using a black windchime. As career is also be symbolised by the colour black in figure 5.2.

## 9. OTHERS

The ninth cure, "Others" opens the way to use anything that is appropriate to your culture or situation and which generates chi, helps protect your place, or slows down sha chi.

As illustrated in figure 5.7, a clothes line can be a wonderful chi generator, as can a bird bath or feeder which attracts the movement of birds can generate chi. In fact, anything that symbolically creates movement can be used.

It may not be appropriate in your decor to hang wind-chimes or crystals, but the careful selection of artwork or posters may also be appropriate. For example, in the inner knowledge corner it may be good to put a painting or poster that is symbolic to you of inner knowledge.

If you are wanting a one-to-one relationship and have balanced the negative space of a missing relationship corner, you may like to reinforce the relationship corner of your bedroom with a poster of a loving couple or objects like two candles, or two teddy bears. These universal symbols of partnership reinforce your intent in the one room which is your private space - your bedroom.

This technique has worked for many clients, who although living in "square" houses or apartments could not find the steady relationships they were seeking. The interesting observation about many of these clients homes, and in particular the relationship corners, was that they often also had symbols of single people, pictures of their children or parents, in these corners, who were symbolically blocking any chance of a relationship.

Similar principles can be applied to any of the sections of the bagua.

## SUMMARY

The Nine Basic Cures generate, anchor, deflect and absorb chi. The ninth cure "others" opens the door for the lateral and symbolic applications of these principles in ways that are appropriate to your lifestyle, culture and decor.

Sometimes it is not one cure that makes a difference, but a combination of cures. During the two weeks after a consultation, at home where no particular corner was missing, the client's two ex-boyfriends came back into her life, and she was able to resolve outstanding issues amicably. One of them commented on how much she had "changed". Also her twenty-year old daughter's "negative" boyfriend uncharacteristically came to the home for the next three days and suddenly stormed out on the third day never to be seen again! His last comment was that he couldn't stand the place anymore. (The daughter was relieved). Unbelievably, the shower drain unblocked to allow water to drain away, instead of flooding the bathroom floor as it had done for the previous twelve months, despite the efforts of the plumber. Coincidences? Apply these cures or corrections to your home or business and decide for yourself.

**Exercise**

Look in one room of your home on the basis of the bagua sections, and then check the objects you have placed in these corners and what they symbolise to you. However, whatever you do, don't fill every corner of your house with "appropriate" symbols; only make adjustments in one corner of one room for something that you feel is lacking in your life, and then observe any changes that may result from this change.

# 7

# Classic Feng Shui Concepts & Rules

## 1.INTERIOR DESIGN & FURNITURE LAYOUTS

Feng shui is also known as "the art of placement". In the larger sense, this can be the placement and location of a building in the landscape, or with interior design it can be the placement of furniture and fixtures within the building. Once furniture is located in a general position that feels comfortable, then subtle corrections to the position of furniture may make a difference to the flow of chi within a place, and thus to the feng shui balance.

This art of placement is what some Western educated people would do naturally; it is usually about "keeping control" in a particular room or situation, and about feeling comfortable. However, when a place is out of balance geomantically, people often move the furniture around constantly, because they intuitively know it doesn't feel right. By applying the feng shui principles discussed in this book, this restless movement of furniture can be reduced, as the place will "feel right".

The idea of the art of placement is also tied to the idea that energy or chi should not flow in straight lines (sha chi). The idea of sha chi or "daggers of energy" can be seen in the way we lay out desk positions in offices.

In an office layout, it is important to be able to see the door of your office so that you are not "stabbed in the back" with "arrows" or "daggers" of chi. People have been intuitively setting up their workspaces this way for a long time and it is one of the many "common sense" applications of feng shui. The classic location for a desk in an office is illustrated below. Its "exact" location can also be affected by many other detailed design factors .

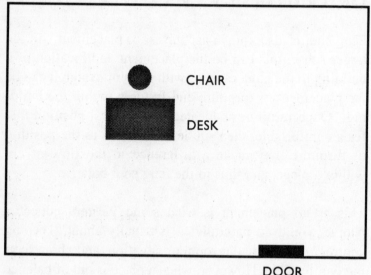

*Figure 7.1 Classic Desk Location*

However, if it is impossible to move your desk and your back is facing the office door, then you might try using a "bright" object from the Nine Basic Cures, which if placed on your desk allows you symbolically to see the door. The bright object might be a crystal, small make up mirror or a mirror framed picture. Usually you do not have to see the door in the reflection but the intent of symbolically viewing the location of the door may be sufficient to improve your comfort.

Similarly, if you are in an open office situation, it is not always possible to see the "front door" or to protect your back, so you can make these adjustments to help you feel more comfortable. If your back is exposed, and people approach you from behind while you are concentrating, then you may become suddenly "frightened". The concept of "frightening" people can be compared with a daydreaming experience. While daydreaming, a person's spirit body tends to separate from their physical body. So if someone frightens them by approaching from behind or while they are daydreaming, it often takes a while to gather their thoughts and feel grounded again, as their spirit body is trying to realign with physical body. Often children exhibit this disjointed feeling if they are woken from a deep sleep. Their spirit and physical bodies are taking time to realign. Adults commonly best associate that feeling with their time at school. If you were daydreaming by looking out the window, and the teacher suddenly frightened you, it took a little while to really feel present in the class room. Chinese philosophy and feng shui give an explanation of how these feelings work and why people often want to protect their backs from attack.

The idea goes right back to the concepts discussed in chapter four. In the classic diagram of the external landscape ( Figure 4.2) with a large mountain at the back and two medium sized mountains on the sides of the site, the home or grave site was protected. The same principles can be applied in many different situations.

Another aspect of office design which should also be considered is the individual requirements of any occupant. It is always best for someone to personalise their office with furniture layouts and decorations which appeal to them and make them feel comfortable. People will usually be more productive if they can arrange the furniture in their office space to suit their particular way of working. They should also put a personal stamp on the space with decorations such as posters, paintings, plants, certificates or colours which make them feel comfortable.

For the greatest impact the layout of these items should also emphasise the feng shui principles of the bagua appropriate to that persons idea of fame, career etc. Again don't overdo this emphasis on the various bagua sections but highlight one or two with objects that appeal to you and symbolise the appropriate bagua symbol. Often good office design provides a simple practical base on which to add the personal decorating touch in offices as well as homes.

Once the general location of the furniture is fixed, based on "protecting our backs" and feeling comfortable, then the subtle movement of furniture, sometimes only by a few centimetres can be applied to any layout. Such movement is often based on intuition and experience.

## Positions of Power - Boardrooms and Dining Rooms

The premise of keeping control by retaining the most powerful position is also seen clearly at the boardroom table in the office or at the dining table in the home. If all other factors are equal, then the strongest position is usually at the head of the table, furthest from the door.

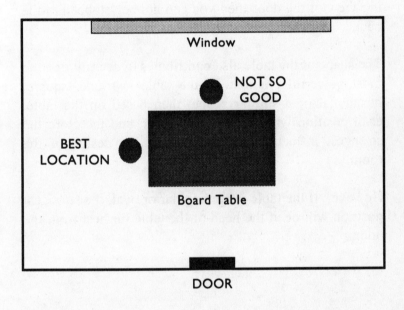

*Figure 7.2  Boardroom Seating Positions*

Other design factors in the room will also normally have a large effect on the positions of power in the room.

Again the aim is to protect the back, and have a direct view of the door. If you want the power position, don't have a window behind your back. Instead, choose a solid wall. When you speak, people will focus on you, not the view through the window. Also if you have a commanding view of the door then you can not be "stabbed in the back"

The shape of the table also contributes to determining the most powerful position. If the table is round, square, hexagonal or a similar shape, then based on the table, each position will be of equal power, and therefore the strongest influence will come from the design of the room.

However, if the table is rectangular or oval, the strongest position will be at the head of the table furthest from the door.

**Dining Room Layouts**

Similarly, in the home the seating positions around a dining room table can have an impact on family meal dynamics and the power roles in the home.

In a male-dominated house the man will often take up the classic head of the table position, however all the factors cited in the boardroom situations above should also be noted. Life is so variable that it is not always logical to apply the rules based on old ideas. Always think out your current situation before blindly instituting a feng shui "rule."

Here is an interesting suggestion regarding the allocation of seats at the dining table. When teenagers begin to rebel against parental power and authority, have them sit in the power positions, talk to their parents, and chew their meal slowly.

Similarly at a dinner party it might be advantageous to place a domineering and loud guest with their back to the door, and a quiet, introverted guest in the power position. This will help balance the chi at the table and allow for an agreeable balance of people and their energies.

The dining room is where people eat food or take in chi to keep the energy flowing in bodies. A pleasant energy in this room will assist the food to be absorbed and digested in a non-stressed way.

This relationship between the food we eat and our chi is particularly evident in the layout of the kitchen. The hot

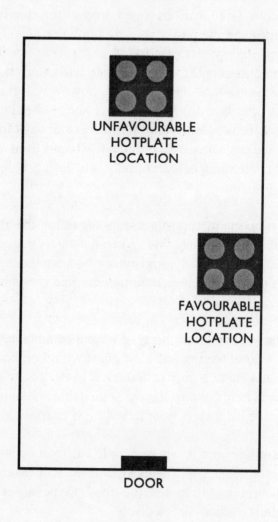

UNFAVOURABLE
HOTPLATE
LOCATION

FAVOURABLE
HOTPLATE
LOCATION

DOOR

*Figure 7.3  Hot Plate Locations in a Kitchen*

plates or stove need to be located where you can see the kitchen door. This allows you to feel secure while cooking.

If you are disturbed or perhaps angry or resentful while cooking, then your disturbed chi is transferred into the food and this is not good for the people who then eat this food.

When you cook food, you should be relaxed, so that your chi, or energy, which is transferred to the food, is also relaxed.

What do you do if your stove or hotplates are in a position that cannot be changed as shown in the diagram above? Go back to the Nine Basic Cures.

If a symbolic bright or shiny object is located near the stove, you will be able to see the "front" door of the kitchen. It may not be appropriate to put a mirror over your stove, but a shiny pot or wok may be hung in this location, or a feng shui crystal located here, or any other item that allows you to symbolically see the door from your cooking position.

## Bed Locations

Another classic application of these principles is the location of beds in a bedroom. The best location for the bed is in a position that allows a clear sight of the bedroom door as indicated by the following diagrams.

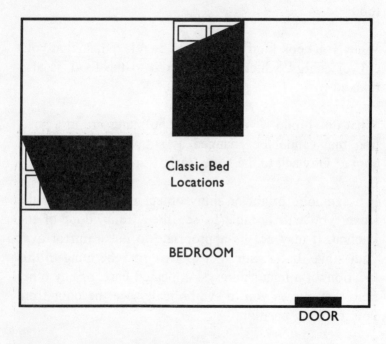

*Figure 7.4  Classic Bed Locations*

It is important to note that the one position not to place a bed is directly opposite the bedroom door, as this is known as the "coffin position" in feng shui. Feng shui recognises this as a position where people cannot get a good nights sleep. Interestingly, many native cultures recognise this position also, as bodies of people are placed in this position just after dying.

## 2. BATHROOM IN THE WEALTH CORNER

One of the classic rules of feng shui which is continually confirmed by people during consultations and lectures, is that if you have a bathroom or toilet in the wealth corner of your home or business, then you are likely to have financial or abundance troubles. It is symbolic of flushing all your wealth or chi away.

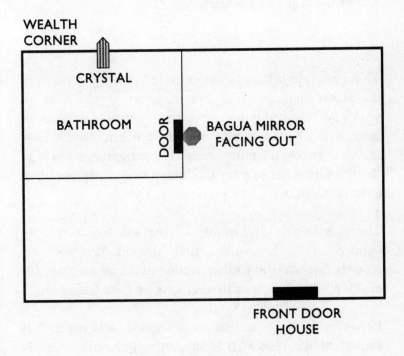

*Figure 7.5  Bathroom in the Wealth Corner*

The classic corrections for the above situation are to:

1. place a crystal in the window of the bathroom to draw in the universal chi,

2. keep the toilet lid closed,

3. keep the door to the bathroom closed,

4. place a bagua mirror above, or on the door, facing out of the bathroom, to seal off this room's energy from the rest of the home or business.

This principle often can be extended to other aspects of the place where we live. For example, if you store all your junk or rubbish in the wealth corner of your block of land, it may have a similar effect by blocking the chi flow in this area. On a smaller scale, if your garbage bin is in the wealth corner of your kitchen, it may be symbolic of a drain in chi, which may affect your wealth.

The classic rule of location of the toilet or bathroom applies only to the wealth corner. You can have your toilet or bathroom in any other section of the bagua and generally not have any negative effects on your life or chi.

However, in any consultation or analysis of a place, it is important to assess what is happening in an overall energetic sense. Sometimes a bathroom in the relationship corner of a home may need correcting, if relationships are an issue and all other aspects of feng shui are balanced. This is not to say that the bathroom location is considered first, but rather it may have a secondary influence on the chi in a place, and intuitively you know it needs balancing. Again, apply all these principles intuitively. There is an infinite combination of circumstances, and one place that is balanced energetically for one person may not be balanced for another whose energy and attitudes to life are different.

## 3. BACK DOOR/ FRONT DOOR

The next classic feng shui rule that affects many people is the front door/ back door rule. If you stand at your "front door" and you can see your "back door", then the chi flowing through your place will be too fast, unless you locate items along the way which slow it down. People who do not slow down the chi flow in this situation often experience everything flowing out of their lives. They do not seem to be able to hold onto anything, be it wealth, relationships or employment.

The traditional way to modify and slow down the chi flow is to place a windchime part the way along the flow. This slows and "curves" the chi, rather than acting like an arrow of sha chi.

The important idea to note is that the rule may apply in many situations, not just your physical front door to back door. It may also apply when standing at your front door you can see a large floor to ceiling type window on the back wall of a house.

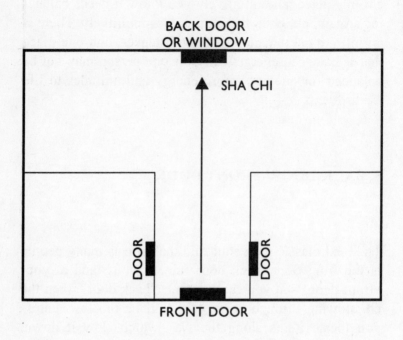

*Figure 7.6  Back Door / Front Door Rule*

It can also apply in the way a house is located on a block of land. If the chi goes straight past the front door, as indicated in figure 5.4, a cure may be needed near the front door to gather chi.

There are any number of examples of this situation, and even though feng shui provides wonderful principles and rules, your observation and adjustment of any place needs to use a lateral approach to the assessment of problems and corrections.

## 4. STAIRS OPPOSITE FRONT DOOR.

Another situation that causes things to flow out of peoples lives occurs when the stairs in their home or business are directly opposite the front door. It is as if everything flows out and can not be contained. The corrections for this situation includes plants, windchimes, a chandelier, a mirror facing the stairs or furniture. If these corrections are placed between the front door and the foot of the stairs they will slow the chi and remove the effects of sha chi.

## 5. MIRRORS

In the previous chapter, the importance of mirrors was highlighted by their power to bring into balance areas with negative space. The power of mirrors can never be underestimated. People have a tendency to be unable to walk past a mirror without looking into it. Whether this is vanity or the light reflective quality of mirrors doesn't matter. People react to mirrors. The way they react can partly be explained by the following examples of the uses of mirrors.

### Front Door Mirrors

They can also be used to protect a place by repelling negative energy. In Western interior design it is common to put a large mirror near and facing towards the front door to intuitively protect the "mouth of chi". In Asia it is more common to put a bagua mirror over the front door to keep away the evil spirits.

*Figure 7.7 Bagua Mirror*

What if you cannot put a bagua mirror or an ordinary mirror near your front door, as neither of these solutions appeals to your design sense or are appropriate in your place? For example, you may live in a federation-style house. Go back to the basics and understand that symbolically the home or business needs protection near the entrance. So why not put something reflective near the front door, that is appropriate to your decor? Maybe a brass door knocker might be more appropriate at the front of a federation-style house or a reflective painting or another cultural symbol of protection which is appropriate to your idea of protection from the outside world.

**Noisy Neighbours**

Mirrors provide an ideal method of reflecting back towards the place where it originated, "chi" which is disturbing your place. Sometimes with amazing results.

Some clients have been able to send back the negative "vibes" and noise of the next door neighbours or their barking dogs by facing mirrors towards these people and their places. The mirror solution may not always give one hundred percent success, but people have observed changes to their neighbours' noise patterns, which cannot be explained by any logic. Often it is only a small mirror facing in their neighbours direction which has adjusted the flow of chi or energy in the form of noise. It may be worth experimenting to see if it helps your noise problem.

It may also be appropriate to use a convex style mirror which instead of reflecting the negative chi, will actually disperse the chi.

**Mirror Wardrobes and Walls**

Many modern houses and apartments have been built with large panels of mirrors on the walls, and in particular with mirrored wardrobe doors. These look great in daylight hours as they create a wonderful feeling of space in some rooms. However, from an energy point of view, they generate a lot of chi which may not be appropriate or desirable in a bedroom when you are trying to calm down and go to sleep.

From the perspective of traditional feng shui, when we go to sleep at night, it is believed that our physical body needs to rest, while our spirit body dreams or goes astral travelling. If however, you have a mirror at the end of your bed, when your spirit body leaves your physical body, it sees a reflection of itself in the mirror and gets frightened, and may immediately rejoin your physical body. Therefore, your physical body does not get a good night's sleep. Whether this is an explanation that is acceptable to your beliefs or not, many people who sleep badly, or who are not "morning" people, are found to sleep opposite mirrors, or in rooms full of mirrors or mirrored wardrobes. They often report improvements to their energy levels and sleep patterns when the mirrors are covered or removed from the bedroom. So if you don't

sleep well and have mirrors in your bedroom, try covering them and see if this makes a difference. There can
never be a complete guarantee with any of these feng shui
cures, but in most cases, people do notice some benefit.

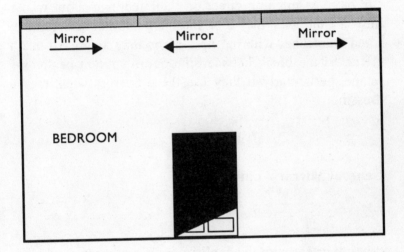

*Figure 7.8 Mirror Wardrobes*

If you travel frequently and sleep badly while you are
away from home, next time you are in a hotel room,
check if there is a mirror opposite the end of the bed. If
so, cover it up or move the bed, and see if it makes a difference to your quality of sleep. (In the Appendix B
details of other energies such as electricity which may
also be disturbing your sleep). Remember that feng shui
can be applied to whatever situation you find yourself in.

## Mirror Tiles

Another application of mirrors in recent years has been the use of mirror tiles. Unfortunately, mirror tiles applied to walls split the chi or energy of the person looking into them, and so cause your image to be "split". It is almost like an image of people with multiple personalities. For this reason it disturbs the self-image of the person and can have an ongoing effect on their feelings about who they are and what they look like. On a larger scale, mirrored wardrobes with multiple doors may also have this effect, as the break between the doors splits a person's image, particularly if they use these mirrors when they dressing.

## General Mirror Applications

It is important with the application of any mirrors which are regularly used in a home to be able to see a whole image of oneself, not a split image. So in bathrooms, for example, the mirror should be sized and located where everyone in the house from the smallest to the tallest person can see, without having to stand in an uncomfortable position, at least the whole image of their face.

From the various applications of mirrors discussed above, it is clear that the use and location of mirrors within any place should be carefully considered. They can have a major impact on the flow of chi in a place and on the chi of the people in that place. Use mirrors wisely.

## 6. BEAMS

Beams often create a cutting chi which can affect people who spend time under the beam, or the beam can act as a block to the flow of chi within a place. Whether a particular beam is causing cutting chi or blocking the flow of chi can quickly be tested by using a dowsing rod or pendulum (see Appendix D). Generally the impact of the beam is dependent on the height of the ceiling and size of the beam.

Commonly, a beam across an opening between two rooms may block the flow of chi. The traditional cure for this is to hang a bamboo flute, with the mouth piece facing down, at a 45 degree angle in each corner that the beam makes with the adjoining wall.

It is not appropriate to hang bamboo flutes in every decor situation, so try to be flexible in the application of these principles. The hanging of other basic cures such as crystals, mobiles, windchimes or bells may be appropriate, or you may be able to hang a basket of flowers or a plant from the beam. In a consultation with a city hotel, a series of beams was blocking the energy from flowing into a "nightclub" type room, so down-lights were located either side of the beams and then the chi flowed easily within the place.

In some styles of houses and offices, large exposed beams are used to give an earthy feel. Often they are not a problem if the ceiling is high, since this minimises the cutting effect of the cutting chi. The cutting chi dissipates, the further away from people the beams are located. However, the effect can be verified quickly with a dowsing rod.

In some rooms, notably ground floor areas of two-storey houses, if the ceilings are low and flat and there is a series of exposed beams, then the beams may cause all sorts of problems. If these rooms are places where people spend a lot of time, then this cutting chi may make them feel uncomfortable, and if beds are located under the exposed beams, this may eventually lead to some physical problems. The only practical solution to this situation is to cover the beams with either painted plasterboard or to hang material, or "sail" cloth, or cotton sheets along the beams, particularly in areas where people either sleep or work at a desk. People who spend time in these type of areas often cannot settle in one place for very long, or they may not sleep well. If you have tried everything else, then it may be the beams causing the problem, so try one of these solutions, and see if there is an improvement.

Another situation to consider is in A-frame houses with exposed beams. If you have your bed located close to the roof/wall, then the beams could be affecting your health. One client suffered from stomach pains whenever he slept in his bed. There was an exposed beam passing directly over his stomach. He received relief when we moved the bed away from the roof/wall of his A-frame house.

Feng shui also counsels never to align your double bed so that a beam sends cutting chi down the centre of the bed, as this will tend to "split the relationship".

## 7. DOORS

Doors are seen as the entrance of chi for any place. A building, house or room takes in its chi through the doors and, to a lesser extent, the windows. If the doors are too small, then not enough chi will get into a place, and conversely if a door is too large, too much chi will get into a place. Whether a door is too large or small, will depend on the use of the space to where the door leads and the proportions of the exterior wall in which a door is located. Also the main door for a building would normally be larger than the internal doors.

Too many doors down a long corridor may affect and confuse the flow of chi. If the doors don't line up opposite each other, then your "vision" can also be split between a long and short view as you leave a room and enter the corridor. Another general rule about doors is when two door handles clash arguments may occur in the household. The correction for this is to wrap a short length of red ribbon around each of the door handles.

## 8. LANDSCAPE AND PLANTS

In the chapter on Nine Basic Cures, the value of plants and landscape was explained in general terms. However probably the most important aspect to consider when selecting plants or trees is their overall shape and the shape of their leaves.

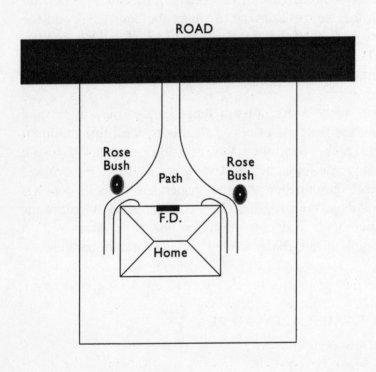

*Figure 7.9  Rose Bushes on Front Paths*

Long spiky leaves send out daggers of sha chi, which tends to unsettle the energy in any place. Now this is fine if you are using these plants as protection for yourself or property, but it is not so good if you place a spiky plant in the relationship corner of your bedroom. You may find that your relationships are always unstable. If you place a spiky plant near the front door of your business, you may not get many customers coming in the front door.

A traditional concept within feng shui is that if you plant spiky plants or rose bushes with thorns (remember it's the symbolism that is important) along your front garden path, then you are unlikely to get many visitors. The strange thing is that this happens regularly in the layout of some gardens and the people can't understand why no one comes to see them. When they move the spiky plants, things suddenly change and they receive more visitors. This is not to say that spiky plants and roses are bad, but that they should be used carefully in any landscape.

In the layout opposite you can see how a home owner intuitively stopped people from going around the back of her house by placing rose bushes on her side footpaths. Everyone always knocked on the front door.

The other more positive aspect of plants is the use of rounded-leaf plants. These are a more beneficial symbol from a traditional feng shui perspective. The shape of plants and trees is also important in that tall thin trees may, like a church steeple, introduce the element of fire and generate too much chi.

# 9. EXISTING REMEDIES AND THEIR EFFECTS

In any assessment of a place, it is important to consider any existing remedies and  the affect they are having on the flow of chi. You may have intuitively placed chi corrections in the right places, but it is important to review what impact windchimes, crystals, paintings, posters, furniture, etc, are having on your place. Indeed, you may even decide that by some subtle rearrangement of these items, the chi flow will improve sufficiently and you may not need to apply any other corrections at the time of your first review.

## SUMMARY

These classic concepts and rules are probably easy to understand in most situations, however it is always important to study the chi flow, blockages, symbolism and what people really want from a place, before making corrections. Like everything else these rules can only be general guidelines and for every rule there are exceptions. In the end we need to trust our intuition and apply them in ways that reflect the decor of our home or office.

Remember, treat the application of feng shui as a large personal experiment to observe the changes that occur in your life and don't always expect instantaneous results. Make adjustments slowly and then observe what impact they have on your place. Every place is different and the way you apply the changes has to resonate with your ideas and intuition to make a place feel good. Sometimes just one simple correction will make a huge difference to your life.

**Exercise**

Review each of the concepts in this chapter in terms of the place where you are living now, a place where you have lived previously or a friends home and see if any feng shui patterns emerge from yours or your friends life experiences.

# 8

# Clutter, Energy & Maintenance

## CLUTTER

The role of clutter has an important place in traditional feng shui as clutter has a major affect on the flow of chi in any place. Clutter is not necessarily mess, but more specifically items that we own which have passed their "use-by" date in terms of our need to hang onto them. People tend to hoard material objects for a rainy day, just in case they might be needed. Unfortunately this hoarding of material possessions blocks the flow of chi at home, work, and life in general.

You only need to reflect to a time when you last moved home (and cleared out the junk first), or did a spring clean, to remember the feeling of release, or lightness that accompanies a good clearing out.

A common example of clutter maybe clothes that have not been worn for three or more years, but are being saved just in case they come back into fashion. It is unlikely to or if it does they won't fit. These clothes only clutter our lives and focus our thoughts on the past instead of the present and the future. We need to live in hope, not fear. People who live in fear often are stuck in the past and have difficulties planning for the future. By removing clutter and spring cleaning what is no longer required in their lives, individuals can free themselves of possessions which may have been symbolically and practically weighing them down.

One of the important things to remember is that the "use by" date for the same object maybe different for different people and that the need to do this cleansing of clutter should be done at times and a rate that suits the individual. It involves a continual process of assessment of what is important to someone. So if your life is feeling stuck, look at the things you have around you. What is restricting your growth? What don't you really need any more? Just the simple act of releasing your clutter can have a dramatic affect on your own sense of well-being.

The impact of clutter can be felt when you move home. Often people give "clutter" to the local charity shop. (One person's trash is another person's treasure, so sometimes it may be more appropriate to donate it.) and hire rubbish bins to dump all the half-full cans of paint and other junk. On moving to the new house, they feel a sense of freedom that was due to more than just the move to new surroundings. It was caused by the unburdening of all the junk and clutter.

However, we shouldn't *have* to move every few years. We just need to be honest with ourselves as to what material possessions are important. This is not to advocate a complete minimalist approach, but rather we keep only those things that provide good memories, that are used most of the time and that will be needed during the next year or so. Anything else is likely to be clutter. A simple question to ask about any object is "have I used this in the past twelve months and am I likely to use it again in the next twelve months?" or if "I had to move home or office in one month is this object important enough to take the trouble and pay the cost of moving it?"

## ENERGETIC APPROACH

Some objects seem to have a memory of the times and places in which they have been, and they emit that atmosphere or energy into their current environments. If those objects radiate a negative energy, they can have an dampening effect on our lives. Take care to recognise the impact objects can have on your life.

Many objects bring back great memories, however every so often you may recognise an object which raises negative memories or feelings, and which is indeed clutter in your life. These objects should be released first. In these matters, listen to your intuition. If something makes you feel uneasy, recognise the feeling and remove the object from your surroundings. Over time see if it makes a difference to the atmosphere of your home or business.

Examples of this concept sometimes emerge during consultations, when objects which people have received are having a dramatic affect on their lives. In one case a woman who was having relationship problems suddenly realised during a consultation that the handmade eiderdown she had been given as a wedding present from her mother-in-law was affecting her relationship to her husband. She had intuitively not liked it, but had not connected this reaction with the problems she and her husband had, with a reportedly manipulating woman. It was as if the mother-in-law was in bed with the couple all the time! Her relationship with her husband improved soon after she removed the energetic clutter and replaced it with something that was representative of her own energy - a new eiderdown.

Don't put in pride of place objects that make you feel uneasy, just so that when your friend or Aunt Mable or mother-in-law visit your home, they will see them displayed. Sell them, lose them, give them away or use whatever excuse you like to whoever gave them to you. In the end, you are the person spending a lot of time in your place and you need to have positive things around you that make you feel good, not negative things that energetically drain you or make you feel uncomfortable.

Also consider the objects you have bought. Have you bought clothes, craftwork or furniture from a second hand shop? Stop and consider the background energies that may have been collected by any object.

A classic example of this problem occurred with a very good looking client who had bought a second-hand wardrobe with a full-length mirror in the door. She had always felt inadequate when looking into the mirror, but thought it was her problem. Intuitively, we felt that the wardrobe had been owned by a very old lady, who had watched her beauty disappear before her eyes. She had filled the mirror with this negative energy idea of her image over years, so that the client was feeling this negative image every time she looked into the mirror. In the weeks after the consultation, the client felt better about herself and received many comments from friends about how well she looked.

If something intuitively gives you mixed messages, consider whether the energy beyond its physical appearance could be causing problems to you.

## MAINTENANCE

Clutter, in feng shui terms, can also accrue due to a lack of maintenance on our physical surroundings. If people live in a run-down, ramshackle house with peeling paint and clutter all around them, the place will have strong impact on their chi and their ability to enjoy life. Most people don't live in this extreme situation, but they may have things around them that are not in good repair.

Sometimes the simplest maintenance of your home can make a large difference to your feeling for that place. A simple example of this principle involves light bulbs. If you have broken light bulbs in various sections of your home or business, they may be in a bagua area which is symbolically reflecting a problem in an aspect of your life. Similarly cleaning the windows of your place may "clear your vision of the world".

If a house has rising damp, mould or a leaking roof, then the location of these problems may symbolically represent the areas in the owner's life which are out of balance, based on the bagua layout. Sometimes a crack in the relationship corner of a window pane or mirror can symbolise the relationship problems the people are experiencing. This is not to say that everyone with cracked mirrors or windows has relationship or wealth or other problems. But it is another area of the symbolism represented by feng shui in the material world, and it should be considered when assessing the flow of chi through a place.

One client with "relationship", "career" and "helpful people" problems had mould on her ceilings in these locations based on the bagua layout of her house. The problem was caused by inadequate downpipes, which, during storms, overflowed back into the ceilings of her house. The solution was to install more downpipes with overflows so that the water did not create the mould.

When assessing the feng shui of any place consider the maintenance and physical condition of the property.

## SUMMARY

One of the simplest and most powerful feng shui remedies, and probably the first thing to do even before other
corrections are applied, is to spring clean, remove the
clutter, do the maintenance, clean the dirt and dust from
the home or office. If the task feels too large, do one room
or one cupboard at a time.

Sometimes the objects people have in their homes may
symbolically represent blockages to the flow of chi in
their lives. In any assessment of a home or business, this
possible blockage of the chi flow, should be carefully
considered in conjunction with any other feng shui correction.

**Exercise**

Start your clutter clearing with clothes. Go to one draw or one section of your wardrobe. See if you can select one piece of clothing that you haven't worn for twelve months or you know you won't wear in the next twelve months and give it to a local charity. This clearing of clutter should allow space for a "new" piece of clothing to come into your life. It would be better to remove more than one piece of clothing but we need to start this ongoing process somewhere.

# Conclusion

There are many facets to feng shui knowledge. This book provides a starting point for you to explore some of that ancient knowledge in ways that are applicable to the modern Western lifestyle.

You should not expect feng shui to solve all your problems, however it does provide some interesting concepts which have helped to shape and change peoples lives for many years.

In the application of feng shui remember to trust your intuition and common sense.

May feng shui provide an inspiration to observe your environment in new ways.

# Appendix A

# Associated
# Feng Shui Concepts

## THE FIVE ELEMENT THEORY

In conjunction with feng shui, the five element theory helps to explain further developments of the two dimensional concepts discussed previously. The five element theory is based on the productive and destructive associations of the five chinese elements of our environment.

The Chinese elements are fire, earth (or soil), metal, water and wood (or tree). By way of contrast, the four elements in western culture originating from Greek philosophy are fire, air, earth and water. Why five in the Chinese system?

This can be explained by considering the differences. The Chinese have metal which may be thought of as symbol-

Appendix A

ising the man-made things on earth, and wood, the natural vegetation covering the earth, but no air as it would appear that "water" symbolises the liquid, solid and gaseous (water vapour would be symbolic for air) states of water.

The Chinese system is also seen as a cyclic system of growth and decay compared with the other Greek-based elemental system which is more static. The cyclic nature of the five element theory has two distinct patterns a production cycle and a destruction or control cycle.

**The Production Cycle**

The diagram opposite shows that Wood feeds or produces Fire, that Fire produces Earth, that Earth produces Metal, that Metal produces Water, Water produces Wood.

This cycle is a continuous loop with no beginning or end. The fire-to-water part of the cycle is contracting and the water-to-fire part of the cycle is expanding.

The changes in the growth cycle can represent many things in the world around us. This includes the day-to-night cycle, and the yearly cycle of the seasons. So things become more yin as we head from summer(fire) to winter (water), and more yang as we head from winter(water) to summer(fire).

146

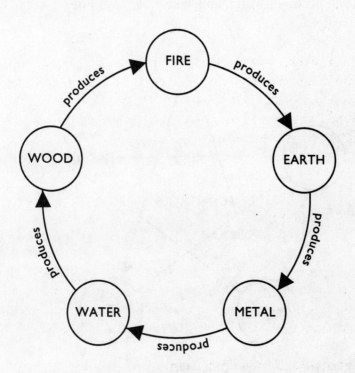

*Figure A1  The Production Cycle*

**The Destruction or Control Cycle**

Fire controls and destroys Metal, Metal destroys Earth, Earth destroys Water, and Water destroys Fire.

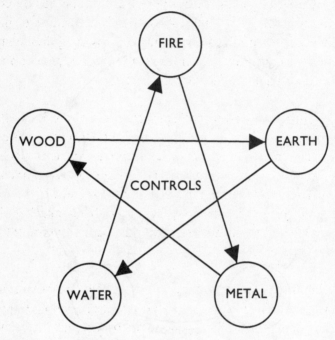

*Figure A2    The Control Cycle*

One aspect of the five element theory can be demonstrated by the relationship between the vertical shapes and the roof types between buildings. For example a "fire type" building like a church with a tall spire would control and destroy a metal type building with a curved roof or shape(from the decay cycle) or complement an earth type building with a flat shape or roof (from the production cycle). Similar relationships between other structures can also be established and form one of the next sections of learning within feng shui.

## I CHING

The I Ching is a Chinese system of divination or advice, similar to tarot cards, runes, American Indian cards or the many other systems which attempt to provide guidance to people who are a little perplexed about what decision to make, and what the future may hold.

The I Ching is based on the eight trigrams of the Early Lo Map formulated by Fu Hsi. These eight trigrams (combinations of three yin and/or yang lines) are turned into 64 hexagrams (combinations of six yin and/or yang lines). The particular hexagram is selected by a system of throwing three coins. The resulting hexagram has a number (1-64), name and various interpretations, depending on what book you then read.

The combination of two trigrams to form the hexagram helps to add definition to the interpretation. For example, the trigram "earth" ☷ over the trigram "heaven" gives hexagram number 11 or "Peace or Tranquillity". Thomas Cleary in his book *The Taoist I Ching* , simply interprets Tranquillity as "The small goes, the great comes. This is auspicious and developmental".

A knowledge of the I Ching can help in further understanding the application of the bagua and feng shui. Like any other system, its interpretation is dependent on the skills of the person asking the question, and on how they then perceive advice. Many of the messages in the I Ching can appear very obscure to a lay person, but after years of practice, a devotee can become quite adept at interpreting the ancient book's wisdom.

## DIRECTIONS - North, South, East and West

One of the theories used by Chinese geomancers working from the principles of the classical school of feng shui and using a luopan, is compass direction. In the methods discussed in this book the compass direction generally has less impact, while intuition and using dowsing techniques are emphasised.

Many of the ideas of direction were developed for various provinces in China and are open to interpretation based on the many topographical features of that region. The application of feng shui compass directions in other parts of the world can be open to incorrect interpretations as the topography, latitude and longitude may be different from the region in China where the classical feng shui rules were established .

The first major dilemma arises with a northern versus southern hemisphere argument of the orientation of the bagua, as the fire element (or fame) probably should point towards the equator. Now this would be fine except that the sun rises in the east in both hemispheres and this would generally be represented by the wood element from the five-element theory or the "family/ancestors" trigram. If you take a little time to twist your bagua layout around for each hemisphere, you will see that many interpretations of the southern hemisphere bagua only lead to confuse the issue.

In addition, various feng shui books available in English don't always agree with the most auspicious directions to place various rooms in a home. One will clearly tell you to put your kitchen in the south-east corner of your house, and another will tell you to put your kitchen in the north-west corner. What appears to happen is that these books are written by practitioners who have been taught by people from various provinces of China. The one who suggests the south-east corner for the kitchen was influenced by the fact that a desert was located to the north-west of this particular home, and as the winds blow off the desert, they carried the sand into the home. It was best to put the kitchen on the protected side of the home away from the desert. Conversely, the practitioner who advised to locate the kitchen on the north-west side of the home had the desert on the south-east side of the home. The whole issue of directions and the most auspicious place to locate various rooms is a real trap for people applying this knowledge in western cultures far removed from feng shui's origins.

Rather than expecting a book to give all the answers on auspicious directions, use intuitive skills to apply the feng shui knowledge to any situation, without becoming to bogged down in what happened in ancient China.

One part of directions which may be important in a particular locality is the orientation of a building and its relationship to the surrounding structures, based on the direction the sun rises and falls in various seasons. Any overshadowing, and whether the front door faces east or west, may have an impact on other corrections you are implementing. The direction the sun rises in relation to your front door or mouth of chi can have an impact on the feng shui balance of a place and on your own chi. It would generally be better to have the door of your house facing east, if you want to increase the yang chi of the place, but not if the place was already overcharged with chi. The whole issue of direction may only confuse someone starting to discover the world of feng shui, so initially it should not be considered in the decision-making about balancing the energy of a place.

## NINE STAR KI ASTROLOGY

Nine star ki is an astrology system which may form a helpful adjunct to feng shui decisions once the concepts of this book have been studied, applied and understood. It is mostly used by the classical geomancer and sometimes by the intuitive geomancer.

It forms another part of Chinese philosophy by reflecting the relationship between heaven and earth. Nine Star Ki or Chinese astrology plays a significant part in Chinese divination. This system proposes that the "heavens" energy affects people.

Nine Star Ki is often used by feng shui masters to determine the most auspicious times and dates for certain ceremonies to occur  such as ground breaking of a new building or opening a new business or when to travel in certain directions, etc.

# Appendix B

# *Electromagnetic Energies*

**THE STORY SO FAR**

Sometimes it is easy to forget how recently electricity and electrical appliances became commonplace. Today, we take for granted all the wonderful benefits electricity brings to modern life. Our homes and offices are full of equipment that uses electricity and sometimes generates electromagnetic fields. Often the equipment is in areas where we spend a lot of time - beds, desks, chairs, etc, What is less well known, and publicised is the health hazards which reportedly may be created by invisible electromagnetic field (EMF),

One of the first research papers about the impact of electromagnetic fields and human health was published in 1979 by Nancy Wertheimer, a Harvard Ph.D. and

University of Colorado epidemiologist. While looking for an environmental link to childhood leukaemia, she noticed electrical transformers on poles outside many of the houses she was visiting. She documented 344 cases of children suffering from cancer/leukaemia and found that a significantly higher proportion than would have normally be expected lived near these transformers, thus indicating a link between leukaemia and location close to these transformers.

At the same time, Robert Becker, M.D. was establishing a link between increases in infant mortality rates when exposed to 60 Hz electric fields (normal household electricity) and Dr. F. Stephen Perry, working in rural England, noticed a higher incidence of mental disturbances and suicide for people who lived near High Voltage (H.V.) power lines.

Dr. Becker also served on a committee of independent experts reviewing a U.S. Navy project code-named "Sanguine". One of the results they found, amongst many others, was "that a one day exposure to the magnetic field component of the exercise produced a significant increase in the serum-triglyceride(s-t) levels in nine out of ten subjects." (s-t levels are increased by a stress response in humans and are related to fat and cholesterol metabolism).

The final report of the committee contained the following statement:

*This committee recommend that the Electromagnetic Radiation Management Advisory Council (a White House Agency) be apprised of the positive findings evaluated by this committee and their possible significance (should they be validated by future studies) to the large population at risk in the U.S. who are exposed to 60 Hz fields from power lines and other 60 Hz sources.*

(In Australia 240 v electrical current operates at a frequency of 50 Hz, which is very similar).

The New York Health/Power Lines Project followed this study with a five-year study which supposedly (based on background information) set out to disprove the above findings. It eventually found that twenty percent of childhood cancers appeared to be produced by an exposure to a 3 milligauss (mg) magnetic field.

Many other studies in recent years have also found that repeated exposure to electromagnetic fields has a biological effect on people. In 1991 a survey found that 10,000 research papers had been published on the subject since 1979, and the growing body of evidence is that EMF's do affect human health. Experts in the scientific world continue to criticise each other's method of experiment and sampling, but the general trend appears to recognise some connection between EMF's and human health.

On May 5, 1994, the European Parliament passed a motion for a resolution that asked member States "to consider a joint interdisciplinary research and standards programme for combating the harmful effects of non-iodizing electromagnetic radiation".

The growing evidence suggests that regular exposure (it is time-related) to EMF's can lead to some minor ailments such as insomnia, disturbed sleep, waking up tired after a long night's sleep or just generally feeling out of sorts. Some of the research indicates that exposure may also be a trigger for more serious problems such as cancer, miscarriage, cot deaths, M.E., depression and suicide. It is important to draw the distinction that EMF's may not necessarily directly cause the disease or illness, but they may potentially affect people's immune system's ability to fight disease.

In his book, *Cross Currents,* (p204), Dr. Robert Becker states:

*All abnormal, man-made electromagnetic fields, regardless of their frequencies, produce the same biological effects. These effects, which deviate from normal functions and are actually or potentially harmful, are the following:*

*-effects on growing cells, such as increases in the rate of cancer-cell division*

*-increases in the incidence of certain cancers*

*-development abnormalities in embryos."*

He also notes that alterations in neurochemicals, resulting in behavioural abnormalities, alterations in biological cycles and alterations in learning ability occur.

To put this into a measurable scientific perspective, Swedish studies up until 1991 recommended that the safe limit for human exposure to EMF was 3 mg. They recently reduced this level to 1 mg. These fields can be measured easily with electromagnetic gauges available from electronic shops.

These standards are set for the majority of the population. It should be noted that peoples' reactions to EMF are all different as their electrosensitivity varies. Some people will find that even 1 mg, is too high while others will find they can be in fields of 10 mg or more and not be affected. Another factor to be aware of is that the intensity of the field may vary over time in different locations. This is particularly evident at different times of the day and year based on the electrical demand in an area.


## SO WHAT DO YOU DO ?


The ultimate recommendation is a policy of prudent avoidance. Stay away from EMF in places where you spend long periods of time - your desk or bed.

To assess your current exposure firstly, consider the wider environment in which you live. Based on some of the studies it would appear that it is not advisable to live near substations or high voltage lines.

A recent client was having major sleeping and personality problems. He only slept two to three hours a night and was constantly hyperactive. On reviewing the EMF in his bedroom it was found that he was sleeping in a field of approximately 25 mg, caused by a major electrical substation, located next door to the house that he was renting.

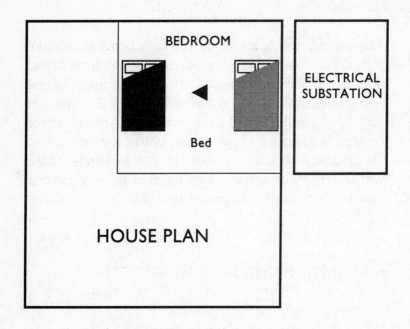

*Figure B1  Substation next to Home*

When he moved his bed to the other side of the room, where the field dropped to 5 mg, he immediately began sleeping eight to ten hours a night and his personality calmed down considerably. It was as if the electromagnetic field was keeping him "switched on" and his body could not get the rest that it needed when he went to bed. After experiencing this change, he moved out of this place to another house (without any substations nearby), and gradually got his life back into order. This example reflects other overseas experiences about the affect major substations can have on people, particularly if they are located close to residential buildings.

## ELECTRICAL SWITCHBOARDS

Unfortunately it is not as simple as staying away from substations and H.V. electrical wires. In our homes and offices having the bedroom next to the main switchboard (MSB) may not be a good idea. The EMF from the M.S.B. does not appear to be stopped by bricks, timber, concrete or plasterboard of the walls. It is common to find EMF levels around 5-10 mg on the internal wall near the MSB. For example if a bed is located next to this wall, then while people are sleeping the EMF from the MSB maybe affecting their bodies as shown in the following diagram.

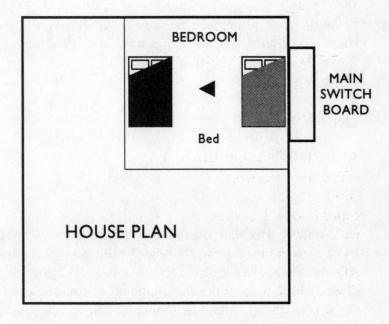

*Figure B2   Main Switchboard  next to Bedroom*

A recent example of this situation involved a 5 year old

boy who could not go to sleep in his bed. He always fell asleep in his mother's or father's lap, in the lounge room, before being placed back in his bed next to the MSB. When the bed was moved to the opposite side of the room, he was generally able to sleep better.

Often an EMF gauge is not needed to show if something is wrong. If children wake up each morning at the end of their beds, then maybe a EMF is affecting them. Children appear to be more sensitive to EMF's and other energies, and careful observation of their reactions to certain places may indicate if any negative energies are affecting them. However, adults also display varying symptoms when their beds are located in the above position. If people wake up tired, grumpy or are constantly getting ill, and they are close to any EMF, it would be a good idea to move the bed and see if it makes a difference to their wellbeing.

## ELECTRICAL APPLIANCES

In the same way that substations and switchboards can have an affect on people and their health, so can electrical appliances which are located near desks, beds or chairs where we spend a large amount of time. The following examples highlight some of the problems in homes or offices.

## Refrigerator in Kitchen next to Bedroom

In the diagram below, an electromagnetic field is generated by the motor of the refrigerator. As the motor switches on and off during the night, the person sleeping in the bed maybe affected.

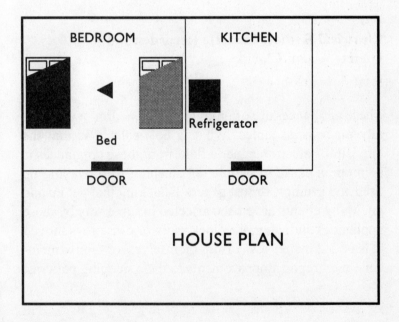

*Figure B3   Refrigerator next to Bedroom*

**Solution**: move the bed to the other side of the room.

## Televisions

Televisions radiate strong electromagnetic fields from their cathode ray tube. The electromagnetic reading at a distance of 30 cm. is usually about 25-30 mg and at 1.2 m (4 feet) often still around 3 mg. The old rule of staying 1.2 m away from television sets probably has some validity considering the influence of electromagnetic fields.

## Electrical Radios, Cassette Recorder and Quartz Alarm Clocks

These appliances are often found in the bedroom and usually on bedside tables. What is not realised is that the "invisible" electromagnetic field from these appliances is a common cause of people not sleeping well, waking up tired and grumpy, or just generally lacking that get up and go. Many clients have been affected in some way by these appliances and when the clock radio or cassette is moved at least 1.2 metres away from themselves, or family members, they report improvements to their sleeping patterns.

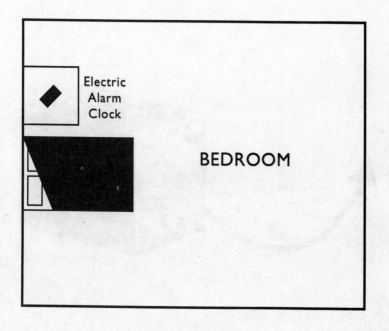

*Figure B4  Electrical Alarm Clock near Bed*

## Transformers

Another problem with electrical appliances is that they sometimes have small transformers which are either located in the appliance or are at the power point as illustrated below.

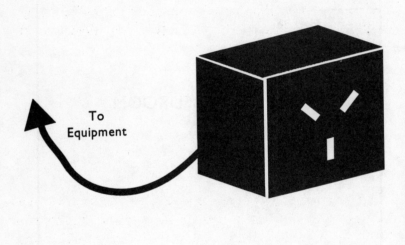

*Figure B5   Black Electrical Transformer*

These transformers transform the main household current from 240 V (in Australia) to 12 V or 6 V, so that the appliance also can operate with batteries. At the point where the transformer is located either at the power point or in the appliance the EMF may be up to 100 mg when they are operating with electricity, but not if they are operating on batteries.

A common occurrence is that parents put small electrical cassette recorders with these transformers next to their children's head and play soothing music for them to go to sleep. However sometimes the children may not be able to sleep if the recorder is placed too close to their heads, due to the field of influence of the EMF.

This concept can be extended to other similarly designed electrical appliances. What's more, even if an appliance is switched on at the power point, and not switched on within the appliance, the electromagnetic field is still being generated in the transformer.


**Battery Chargers**


With the advent of mobile phones and the need to keep charging the batteries, people often locate the battery charger near their beds or desks. The battery chargers work on the same principle as transformers mentioned above, so they also should be placed elsewhere in the home or office.

**Electric Blankets**

Opinions vary widely on the effect of EMF caused by electric blankets as people react to them in many individual ways. The general comment on electric blankets is that if you have one, and you use it, then consider "your" reaction to the blanket. If, after correcting everything else discussed in this book, you still have sleeping problems, then it might be time to get rid of the electric blanket.

Alternatively if you decide you must use an electric blanket, you might take some of the following steps to minimise the effect of the blanket on you. Firstly heat up the bed before you get into it and then pull the plug out of the power point, so that no leakage of electric current gets into the coils of the blanket while you are asleep. For most people electric blankets are not recommended. Try hot water bottles.

**COMPUTER SCREENS**

One of the most common ways that electromagnetic fields affect people today is from computer screens. The electromagnetic field from many computer screens at a distance of around 40 cm., is often between 20-30 mg. (7-10 times the 1991 Swedish safe limit)

In 1991, the Swedish Government introduced a standard referred to as MPR 2, which defines a number of performance specifications for computer screens. One of the

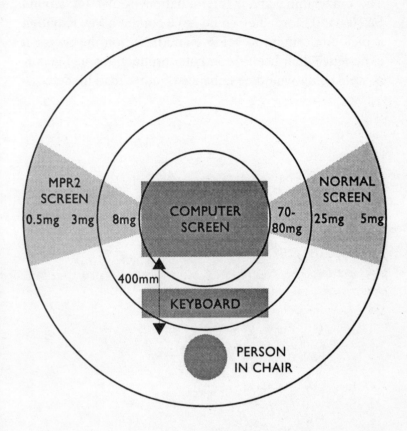

*Figure B6  Computer Screen Plan*

standards states that: "Computer Screens' EMF should not be more than 3 mg at a distance of 400 mm from the screen". Computer screens conforming to this standard are now commonly sold throughout Europe. However, competitive pricing pressures mean that in countries like

Australia, people are still buying old standard screens. The crazy thing about this situation is that for around $A100-150 more, they could have bought a low radiation screen conforming to MPR 2 and based on the Swedish experience their health, computer productivity and general well-being would be enhanced, rather than hindered.

## SUMMARY

The information above is a brief summary of the growing research into the effects of electricity and electromagnetic fields on people. It has the potential to be the next "asbestos type" issue in regard to our health based on overseas research trends. There is a growing body of evidence which supports the notion of "prudent avoidance" of electromagnetic fields.

At this time there is no known scientific way of protecting people from the influence of these fields. Some of the "esoteric" solutions which may work for some people include natural crystals, "purple plates" or live plants, but in the end "prudent" avoidance appears to be the best policy.

# Appendix C

# Natural Earth Energies

## BACKGROUND INFORMATION

Kathe Bachler, an Austrian teacher who became interested in why some of her pupils were more prone to sickness than others, has written the book *Earth Radiation, the Startling Discoveries of a Dowser* which is a best seller in Europe. Currently in its 11th edition, it was translated into English in 1984.

The book contains numerous examples of health problems being linked with earth radiations or natural earth energies. A television program has been made about Bachler's work, and her book was endorsed by Dr. Karl Berg, the Archbishop of Salzburg. The results of her study are confirmed by many different European doctors who often call in energy dowsers, to help reduce the chances of disease in people.

Kathe Bachler has found that all living organisms, plants, animals and humans alike, react in one way or another to these earth energies but their reactions sometimes differ. She found that some plants and animals thrive in the environment that is found above "negative earth energies".

She reported that in the animal kingdom bees, ants and termites build their nests, and mushrooms and many medicinal herbs grow more easily when they are located above negative earth energies.. It has been found that bees produce more honey in these locations. Whereas humans, dogs, most domesticated animals, horses, cattle, pigs, and hens find negative earth energy zones intolerable and therefore instinctively try to avoid them, or if that proves impossible, sometimes become ill.

These conclusions were reached after dowsing 3000 houses and flats involving 12000 people in 15 countries. Similar information was published by Gustav Frieherr von Pohl in the 1930's and more recently by Rolf Gordon of the Dulwich Health Society in England.

The list of diseases which they link with earth radiations includes cancer, aids, arthritis, rheumatism, asthma, M.E., migraines, insomnia, many stomach, kidney, bladder, liver and gall bladder disorders, bed wetting, nervous, emotional and mental disturbances etc. It is not that the negative earth energy causes the disease but that it appears to have an impact on the immune system and maybe a trigger for the diseases.

In Germany some well respected doctors have observed similar results from their studies. The publication *Are you Sleeping in a Safe Place?* by Englishman, Rolf Gordon provides a summary of reported comments by German doctors.

*Ernst Hartman M.D. says that in thirty years of practice, he has not come across a patient with cancer or otherwise seriously ill with the exception of disease caused by bacteria or virus infections who has not slept or stayed for long periods on harmful earth radiation.*

*Arnold Mannlicher M.D. thinks that cancer is a disease of location. He wrote in a Swiss medical Journal that in thirty years in practice, he had not yet found a case of cancer where there was an absence of the influences of the earth.*

*Dr. Hans Neiper In his book Revolution in Technology, Medicine and Society states: "According to studies I have initiated, at least 92% of all cancer patients I have examined have remained for long periods of time especially in respect of their sleeping place in geopathic stressed zones. This does not mean that the geopathic zone, produces cancer, but rather it is the ultimate push button that makes the thing happen."*

*Dr. Hager, President of the Scientific Association of Medical Doctors, with the help of a professional dowser, Privy Councillor C. Williams, checked the houses of 5348 people in the town of Stettin, who had died of cancer and found in all cases that strong earth rays had crossed these homes.*

*Of special interest was a five year survey of three homes for elderly people (retirement villages) in the town. In a home in which strong rays were found, 38 people had died of cancer. In the second home with weak rays, two people had died of cancer. In the home with no harmful rays at all, nobody had died of cancer. In five houses built over particularly strong rays, he found an average of 38 cancer cases over 21 years!*

In essence, what they have found is that people who spend a lot of time in areas located above these energy lines often have health problems. It appears that people's immune systems are weakened when they spend time over these energies and they are more susceptible to health problems. The initial symptoms may only be insomnia, however other symptoms may arise depending on the length of exposure, the intensity of the energy and individual response.

# ONE WAY TO CORRECT EARTH ENERGIES

Many people have various theories about earth energies and how to correct them. The information presented here is one view of methods which have been used to correct these lines. The main method for finding energy lines is a technique called dowsing, which is described in Appendix D.

These energy lines have various names including harmful earth rays, earth energies, earth radiations or geopathic stress, however to simplify the description, the terms positive or negative earth energy are used. When an earth energy is harmful to people, it is a negative earth energy.

In some places positive earth energies already exist in nature and need no correction. Negative earth energies require correction to bring any place into geomantic balance. When they are corrected, they are termed positive earth energies.

**Underground Water Streams**

Dowsers skills have been used for centuries to find water, in underground water streams or fissures, under the earth's surface. Dowsers use a rod to locate the underground water stream relative to their position at the surface of the earth. They can also use a pendulum to find out about the depth of the water, the flow rate, the quality and other things of interest, as these attributes are important to their work in finding suitable water to bore. These underground water streams are found because they generate an energy at the earth's surface, which appears to have a biological affect on people. It is the dowser's sensitivity to this energy that allows it to be found.

However it is not only dowsers who are sensitive to this energy, but many living organisms, as described earlier by Kathe Bachler. If the underground water stream produces a negative affect on people who live above this energy, then this water stream is usually referred to as a "black stream" or a "negative earth energy". The aim of dowsing for underground water streams in any home or business is to find negative energies and correct them.

While rod dowsing a place, the following can be asked: "Please show me any underground water energies which are causing problems to the health of the people in this place." This procedure can be used to dowse the any place to find out if you find any underground water energies causing problems. Please note that these questions aim to give a guideline as to the dowser's intent. As you become more proficient at dowsing, you will find words and methods that may suit you better.

A classic example of problems which negative underground water streams can cause occurred during recent consulting work. The idea of one water stream passing under a bed is usually pretty bad, but to have three streams intersecting

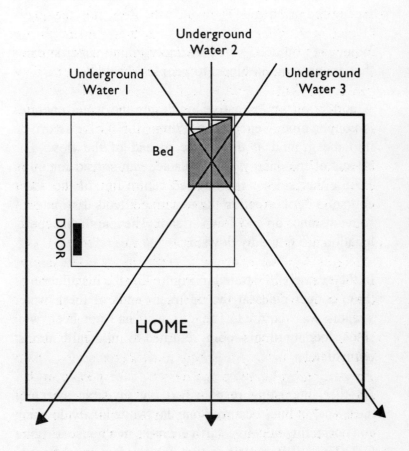

*Figure C1  Underground Water Example*

under a child's bed was pretty dramatic, particularly since both she and her sister had been sick over the years when they slept in this particular bedroom.

It would appear that the intersection point creates a vortex and amplifies the energies which, if they are negative may make people who spend a lot of time at or near this place tired or unwell.

What can you do if you find underground water streams that are causing problems to peoples' health?

A correction for "negative" underground water energies is copper pipe. Generally a 12mm (0.5") pipe is driven into the ground at the upstream end of the flow. The effects of the energy at the surface can spread for up to 1.5m either side of the dowsed centre line of the water course. After correction the negative affects dissipate for some distance up and down stream. The length and "best" location are found by dowsing.

In the example illustrated in Figure C1, the installation of three copper pipes at the upstream ends of these water streams was required. The girl who had not been well since sleeping in this room, returned to full health almost immediately.

Another interesting response to the invisible affect of these energy lines occurred one day while busily dowsing and correcting negative earth energies in a house. (Figure C2) The client explained that her children would never go down the back yard to play under a large willow tree with sand pit and play area. On dowsing the backyard, an underground water stream was found running across the

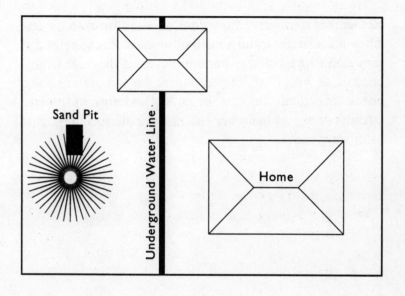

*Figure C2  Underground Waterline in Backyard*

backyard. This needed correcting, with a short length of copper pipe, and by the end of the consultation, the children were playing under the tree and enjoying a sand pit they had previously ignored.

Remember to observe how your children react to places. They are usually quite sensitive to earth energies and if they don't like going to certain places, if they get frightened or, as with EMF, they end up at the end of their beds, check the area out for negative underground water streams or any of the other energies we discuss in the rest of this appendix.

## Step by Step Guide to find and correct Underground Water Energies

1. Find the water stream by rod dowsing.

2. Find the length and number of pipes, which will correct the negative stream by pendulum dowsing.

3. Find the best place to locate the pipes by rod dowsing along the energy line. (Often the rod will spin when you find the appropriate place.)

4. Hammer the pipe or pipes into the ground.

5. Now re-dowse the line to see if:

(a) a negative underground water line exists. The rod should not respond. If it does, recheck to see if further corrections are needed using your pendulum.

(b) a positive underground water line exists. The dowsing rod should respond this time at the same place, where the negative underground water line was previously located. The first time people dowse for earth energies often feels extraordinary. However when people who have been sleeping over these lines, and are not well, notice that they are getting better after making corrections, it is deeply satisfying.

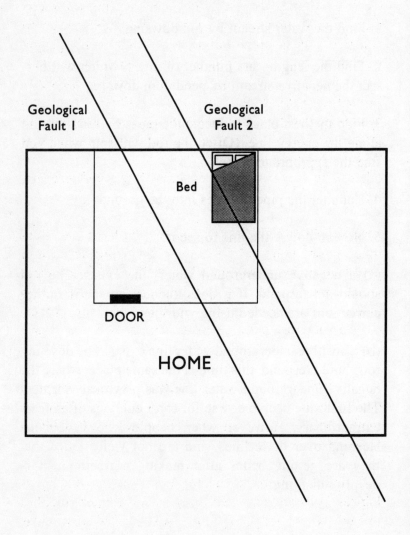

Geological
Fault 1

Geological
Fault 2

Bed

DOOR

HOME

*Figure C3  Geological Faults under Bedroom*

## Geological Faults

Geological faults are commonly found at the earth's surface. The movement of the earth at these faults appears to generate a stress which can trigger disease within people who spend time, near or above these zones. When other earth energies cross geological faults they are often dislocated in ways which can further influence people's health. Geological faults appear to have such a profound influence on the earth's energies surrounding them that they must be the first energies corrected. Then all the other earth energies can be stabilised, mapped and corrected.

An example of the affect these lines can have was illustrated in one house where the seven-year-old boy could not sleep in his bedroom. (Figure C3) Two geological faults were dowsed running through his bedroom, so no matter where the bed was moved he was still being affected. He ended up sleeping in the loungeroom on a mattress.

After installing the pipe corrections similar to those detailed below, he was able to return to his room and his mother bought him a dog which also slept comfortably in the room.

In a similar way to the underground water streams, geological faults are corrected using 12mm copper pipe, but this time with a length of copper wire twisted a particular number of turns, around the top of the pipe either clockwise or anticlockwise.

**Step by step guide to find and correct Geological Faults**

Find:

1. the fault by rod dowsing.

2. the length and number of pipes, by pendulum.

3 how many turns of wire to each pipe, by pendulum.

4. whether the turns should be clockwise or anticlockwise on the pipe, by pendulum.

5. the best place to put the pipe in the ground, by rod dowsing.

6. whether the energy from the geological fault has changed from negative to positive, by rod dowsing.

It is interesting to note that geological faults and/or underground water streams are often found near most stone circles in England. These were places where people often spent a short time but never lived near them.

## Geomagnetic Lines

The earth's geomagnetic field appears to create a subtle energy which may have a biological effect on people and the fertility of soil in different places. Scientists can measure the earth's magnetic field using instruments which indicate a fairly even magnetic field.

Unfortunately our bodies are more sensitive than any known scientific instrument and we sometimes pick up any variations of geomagnetism in a particular place. This variation may then have a deleterious affect on our bodies with various symptoms apparently triggered by this energy.

This earth energy appears to travel in spirals which may be clockwise or anti clockwise and up to 2m wide. It may also travel in a cyclical up and down motion. The energy can be dowsed for its intensity and frequency as described in the table below (figure C4) which has been developed by a South Australian dowser, Jurgen Schmidt. (Published in the *S.A. Dowsers Assoc. Newsletter*, 1988)

If a line is in harmony, it is shown as a positive intensity in the chart. If a line is out of harmony, it is shown as a negative intensity. The part of the body being affected is reflected in the frequency chart.

The impact is time-based, so to be affected you would need to spend a large proportion of your day in a geomagnetic energy field, say, at a desk or bed.

# FIELD FREQUENCY EFFECTS

| | FREQUENCY RANGE (Cycles per sec.) | TISSUE SENSITIVE TO THIS RANGE |
|---|---|---|
| 1 | 96-320hz | Bone |
| 2 | 321-1200hz | Cartilage, sinuses, ligaments, tendons |
| 3 | 1201-2910hz | Intestines, liver, kidneys, body organs |
| 4 | 2911-4880hz | Nervous system, brain |
| 5 | 4881-11600hz | Lymphatic and circulatory system |
| 6 | 11601-18350hz | Respiratory system, mucous membranes |
| 7 | 18351-33400hz | Meridian system |

# FIELD INTENSITY EFFECTS

| | POLARITY AND INTENSITY | MANIFESTATION OVER TIME |
|---|---|---|
| -1 | -1 to -125mg | Slow disruption over 15 - 25 yrs |
| -2 | -126 to -275mg | Moderate disruption over 8 - 14 yrs |
| -3 | -276 to -675mg | High risk 2 - 7 yrs |
| -4 | -676mg + | Extreme disruption in less than 2 yrs |
| | "NEGATIVE" GEOMAGNETIC LINES INTENSITY | |
| +1 | 1 to 125mg | Background earth field |
| +2 | 126 to 275mg | Energising field - long term (12 months +) |
| +3 | 276 to 675mg | Regeneration field (less than 12 months) |
| +4 | 676 to 1200mg | Healing field - 4 to 10 hours |
| +5 | 1200mg + | Spontaneous healing - 10 minutes |
| | "POSITIVE" GEOMAGNETIC LINES INTENSITY | |

*Figure C4 Intensity and Frequency of Geomagnetic Lines*

The correction for a negative geomagnetic field is a wire circular coil. The number of turns, direction, angle of placement all can be dowsed. The lines will mostly run north to south, but local environmental factors can change the direction.

This energy appears to have an impact on people, as was found when one of these lines was dowsed in the bedroom of a teenage boy who was constantly getting migraines. The geomagnetic line had an intensity of -280 mg. and a frequency of 3500 Hz.. After the installation of the wire coil, the migraines disappeared.

# OTHER GENERAL COMMENTS ABOUT EARTH ENERGIES

## What about Apartments and Multi-Storey Offices?

It would be very difficult to apply some of these corrections in particular copper pipes to apartments and multi-stored offices. Instead, use feng shui cures with intuition and commonsense. Sometimes this will help to change earth energies. Again use your pendulum or rod to check the results.

### Schuman Resonance

Schuman resonance is another energy concept that can be considered in any study of geomancy. It is defined as an energy which is created by a polarity between the earth and the ionosphere. It would appear that the polarity is represented by an electrical charge of approximately 300,000 volts and that the normal resonance at the earth's surface is approx 7.8 Hz. If the frequency of the magnetic field fluctuates as a response to changes in our local environment, then this is termed a Schuman Resonance.

Reportedly the Schuman Resonance concept has been applied to the NASA Space program. They apparently found that when the original astronauts returned to earth, they were disoriented because they were outside the influence of what is termed the Schuman Resonance. In the succeeding manned space flights, scientists artificially generated the resonance and found that the earlier disorientation disappeared.

In the modern world it has been reported that reinforced concrete framed buildings shield out Schuman Resonance. The generation of Schuman resonance appears to be helped by a diversity of tree cover which corrects any energy imbalance. The use of indoor and outdoor plants in buildings and their landscaping may sometimes help.

**Ley Lines**

How do ley lines fit into the above information? It really is a matter of definition. The definition of a ley line is probably one of the widest and most argued terms in geomancy.

The term "ley" is more a generic term for the many different types of lines on the landscape connecting places of common origins, such as sacred sites, churches, grave yards, stone circles, etc.. The term "ley" is for the earth mysteries theorists who are researching the history of these lines. They ask why places like Stonehenge, Avebury, St Michael's Mount, etc. are located on various straight lines in the landscape, rather than study earth energy lines and their affect people today. Some people even refer to earth energies as energy ley lines, but this appears to only confuse the issue. It is easier to leave ley lines to the earth mysteries researchers. One of the major ley lines found in England is called the St. Michael's Line. For people wanting to investigate this side of geomancy, it is an interesting place to start your journey.

## SUMMARY

Various types of earth energies have been dowsed above the earth and appear to have an affect on people's health. The study of earth energies is an area worth investigating in conjunction with modern and traditional medicine, particularly when puzzling symptoms continue after the best medical advice cannot find a solution.

Initially it can be instructive to dowse for each individual type of energy line, however it might not be appropriate once the skill has been developed. It may be more appropriate to generally dowse for negative earth energies which are affecting people's lives and health in this place. In this way it simplifies the quest and can still achieve the same result  finding negative earth energies and either neutralising them or transforming them to positive earth energies.

If earth energies are corrected in association with feng shui adjustments then both elements of geomancy appear to then work more effectively as the total energy of the place has been adjusted.

# Appendix D

# Dowsing

## HISTORY

The art of dowsing has been used to find water, minerals and many other things of interest for thousands of years. The origins of dowsing are lost in pre-history, but Egyptian murals show people holding forked rods, which indicate that dowsing may have been used by man since ancient times. The use of a dowsing rod may not have appeared before these times, as man did not need a dowsing rod, but trusted his intuition about the state of the energies of any place.

In 1556, G. Agricola published an illustrated book *De Re Metallica* with many woodblock illustrations and in particular the one shown below. It shows the stages of dowsing, from cutting a branch to the rod reacting and finding minerals.

*Figure D1   Early Dowsers*

In the early eighteenth century dowsing must have been recognised as it is described in the following verse of Jonathan Swift : ( *Dowsing for Health*, Bailey, p17)

*They tell us something strange and odd,*

*About a certain Magick Rod,*

*That, bending down its Top, divines*

*When e'er the Soil has Golden Mines:*

*Where there are none , it stands erect,*

*Scorning to show the least Respect.*

## WHAT IS DOWSING?

The dictionary defines dowsing as "To throw water over or extinguish", and then suggests "for dowsing rod or divining rod to see (the)divine." Divine means "to make out by means apparently independent of observations and evidence and inference, tell by intuition or magic or inspiration (future events, persons intention, answer to a problem)". A divining rod is defined as "a switch balanced in dowser's hand to betray by dipping the presence of underground water or minerals." Remember that the "mancy" part of geomancy is defined as divination.

In *The Dowser's Workbook* , (Page 11) Tom Graves defines dowsing as "a way of using your body's own reflexes to help interpret the world around you; to find things; to make sense of things; to develop new ways of looking and seeing."

Dowsing is something that most people can do given the right attitude, intent, training and conditions. The two major types of dowsing are rod dowsing and pendulum dowsing.

Rod dowsing uses a forked tree branch or "L" rod. The most common "L" rod is made from a metal coat hanger. The length of each side varies, but a general rod would be 200 mm and 75 mm on each leg. People focus on the end point of the rod, which then leads them in a direction based on a question they ask.

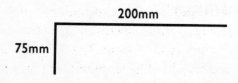

*Figure D2    Typical Dowsing Rod*

Pendulum dowsing consists of holding a solid object suspended at the end of a string and after establishing the direction of movement of your "yes/no" answers, asking questions to see what the response will be.

Dowsing like any other skill, it involves focus and practice. When people dowse, they use the ability of their bodies to feel and react to the subtle earth energies not detected by scientific instruments. Just as no scientific instrument can measure why people instinctively can feel danger or bad vibes, a dowsing rod or pendulum will reflect a person's reaction to subtle earth energies.

## ROD DOWSING

Lightly hold the rod in your hand, state clearly the question that you want answered and then begin a systematic walking pattern over the area where you are dowsing.

The phrasing and intent of your question is particularly important. Consider the differences in the following questions. Are you looking for any underground water line? Or the first edge of an underground water line? Or the centre of an under ground water line? Or any underground water causing health problems? or an underground water that needs to be geomantically corrected so that the place you are at can be harmonised for the highest good of all concerned? They may all give different responses of the dowsing rod in any particular place.

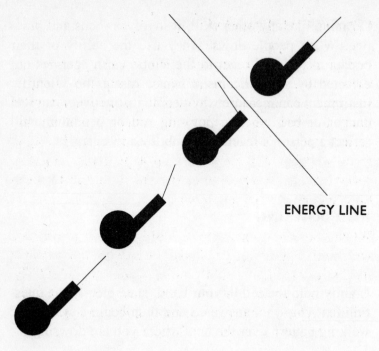

**ENERGY LINE**

*Figure D3   Diagram of Dowsing Rod Movement at an Earth Energy Line.*

When you first start rod dowsing, practice by checking your responses over an object which will give you a known response. A simple test is to walk over a length of water filled garden hose in your backyard and ask to find the water filled garden hose. Then keep building on this skill until you check for energy lines and feng shui chi flows etc. It is only a matter of practice and experience.

If you want to learn this skill and develop it further, there are dowsing societies in various parts of the world and there are often books in local libraries and bookshops which may help.

## PENDULUM DOWSING

Pendulum dowsing can be used to get yes/no type answers to various questions in geomancy. For example, you may want to find out how many underground water lines you need to correct to bring a place into geomantic harmonisation, or is this the front door to apply the bagua from, or what type of correction a particular negative space requires in feng shui or any one of numerous questions that need to be answered.

When you start using a pendulum it is good to practice with simple questions you know the answer to. Questions like is it daytime or night time? Is it dark or light? The more you practice this the more your confidence and skills develop so that you can apply dowsing to feng shui and other questions with confidence.

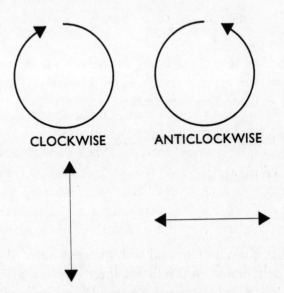

CLOCKWISE     ANTICLOCKWISE

*Figure D4   Possible Pendulums Responses*

It is also good to calibrate on any particular day what is your "yes" and what is your "no" reaction via the pendulum as indicated in Figure D4. These responses can be circular (clockwise or anticlockwise) in motion or they can be a straight line movement (L-R or R-L or Up/ down the page).

Pendulums can be used to ask any number of questions for which all sorts of diagrams have been invented. The rod and pendulum can also help in applying feng shui. Many questions can be framed, such as which corrections which might be needed, what is the front door to an area or mapping the current chi in an area.

## SOME DOWSING TIPS

As our bodies feel these energies, we need to be careful in the way we expose ourselves to the dowsing energy over any extended period of time.

Some of the things to consider are:

### 1. Body Hydration

Our bodies consist of around sixty percent water. If your body is dehydrated, you will get tired very quickly and, as you lose focus, your dowsing results will suffer. Drink lots of water or a water/apple juice combination. The apple juice will help the water be absorbed into the blood stream and hydrate the body quicker and more effectively.

## 2. Kinesiology Balance

Our bodies consist of various meridians of energy. If these get out of balance, we need to rebalance our bodies to ensure the energy is flowing around all the meridians.

In terms of kinesiology, the following techniques are often used:

(a) Rub the "K 27" points

(b) Activate the central meridian

(c) Activate the governing meridian

(d) Rub the eyebrows gently

(e) Cross Crawl

For people not used to these terms there is national and local kinesiology and touch for health associations and practitioners who teach the basic principles of kinesiology in a weekend course. It is a wonderful skill to learn and apply in your day to day life. Another helpful procedure for people who are not aware of kinesiology techniques, is to use a flower essence, Crowea, produced by

Australian Bush Flower Essences which also helps to balance the bodies meridians for some people.

## 3. Focus

A clear focus on the ultimate goal of your dowsing is critical to your success. You should not be in a situation where you can be distracted.

## 4. Relax

It is important while dowsing to stay relaxed. If your muscles are relaxed then the dowsing rod or pendulum will react more reliability.

## 5. Trust your First Reaction

Trust yourself. Don't doubt the results you get as often the more you try to get a particular response, the more confused you may become. If you build your skill slowly at first, with questions and answers you can confirm, then as you start dowsing for answers you don't know, you can trust the results with confidence and without a need to check and recheck your answers.

## 6. Clearly Word Your Questions

Be very specific in the phrasing of your questions. There is a large difference between asking to find an energy line and asking to find a negative earth energy that is affecting peoples health and needs correcting for the overall good of the people in a place.

## 7. Practice

Like most other skills we learn, practice can make a big difference to anyones skills. Try to dowse for everyday answers about your vitamin requirements or food intolerances and then the dowsing for feng shui and geomancy questions which you may be unsure of will be easier to dowse.

## SUMMARY

Dowsing is a skill that can be learnt by most people. It is a great way to start developing your intuition further and to help making feng shui and geomancy decisions. However don't expect your pendulum to answer all life's questions because unfortunately our egos can sometimes cloud the judgement of the way we ask questions and receive answers in using a pendulum. You will find it more reliable and useful as an adjunct to your life if you build the skill slowly over years of practice and observation. Remember, how you word the questions is probably the most important factor.

# Bibliography

Bachler, Kathe, *Earth Radiation*, Manchester, Wordmaster, 1989.

Bailey, Arthur, *Dowsing for Health*, Slough, Quantum, 1990.

Becker, Robert O. M.D., *Cross Currents,* Los Angeles, Jeremy P. Tarcher Inc., 1990.

Coghill, Roger, *Electropollution,* Wellingborough, Thorsons, 1990.

Cleary, Thomas, The Taoist I Ching, Boston, Shambhala, 1986.

Devereux, Paul, *Symbolic Landscapes*, Glastonbury, Gothic Image, 1992.

Eitell, Ernest J., *Feng Shui, or The Rudiments of Natural Science in China*, Hong Kong, Trubner & Co., 1873.

Hean-Tatt, Ong, *The Chinese Pakua*, Malaysia, Pelanduk,1991.

Pennick, Nigel, *The Ancient Science of Geomancy*, London, Thames and Hudson, 1979.

Gordon, Rolf, *Are you Sleeping in a Safe Place?*, London, Dulwich Health Society, 1993.

Graves, Tom, *The Dowser's Workbook*, Wellingborough, Thorsons, 1989.

Heselton, Philip, *The Elements of Earth Mysteries*, Dorset, Element, 1991.

Lonegren, Sig, *Spiriual Dowsing*, Glastonbury, Gothic Image, 1986.

Michell, John, *The New View over Atlantis*, London, Thames and Hudson, 1969, 1972, 1983.

Rossbach, Sarah, *Feng Shui*, London, Rider, 1984.

Rossbach, Sarah, *Interior Design with Feng Shui*, London, Rider, 1987

Smith, Cyril W. & Best, Simon, *Electromagnetic Man*, London, J.M.Dent & Sons, 1989.

von Pohl, Gustav Freiherr, *Earth Currents - Causative Factor of Cancer and Other Diseases*, Stuttgart, Frech-Verlag, 1932 (translated Ingrid Lang 1987).